PORTRAITS IN ROSES

PORTRAITS IN ROSES
109 Years of Kentucky Derby Winners

BEVERLEY BRYANT

AND

JEAN WILLIAMS

McGraw-Hill Book Company
New York St. Louis San Francisco Auckland Bogotá Guatemala
Hamburg Johannesburg Lisbon London Madrid Mexico Montreal
New Delhi Panama Paris San Juan São Paulo Singapore
Sydney Tokyo Toronto

1 2 3 4 5 6 7 8 9 K P T K P T 8 7 6 5 4

ISBN 0-07-008602-8

LIBRARY OF CONGRESS CATALOGING IN PUBLICATION DATA

Bryant, Beverley.
Portraits in roses.
1. Kentucky Derby—History—Pictorial works.   2. Race
horses—United States—History—Pictorial works.   3. Race
horses—Pictorial works. I. Williams, Jean. II. Title.
SF357.K4B78 1984   798.4'3'0976944   83-23872
ISBN 0-07-008602-8

Concept by Jean Williams, Beverley Bryant, and Ken Stuart
Art by Beverley Bryant
Research and writing by Jean Williams
Book design by Roberta Rezk

To Commander Arthur Herbert Bryant, Jr.
1912–1956

B. B.

To Guy Arthur Panero,
who willed this book,

And to William T. Markey,
who lived it.

J. W.

ACKNOWLEDGMENTS

We wish to express our gratitude to the following persons for generously allowing us to reproduce artwork from their private collections.

Mr. and Mrs. Donald A. Fruehling — *Jacket painting: Kentucky Derby,* 1980
Mr. Stephen A. Grove — *Aristides,* 1875
Mr. James Ricciardi — *Ben Ali,* 1886
Mr. Robert Coleman — *Ben Brush,* 1896
Mr. Sanford Bryant — *Pink Star,* 1907
Sovereign Thoroughbreds — *Old Rosebud,* 1914
Sovereign Thoroughbreds — *Regret,* 1915
Mr. W. Cothran Campbell — *Black Gold,* 1924
Mr. James Ricciardi — *Gallant Fox,* 1930
Mrs. Elizabeth Brooks — *Brokers Tip,* 1933
Mr. James Ricciardi — *Lawrin,* 1938
Mr. Peter Henderson — *Hoop Jr.,* 1945
Mr. Michael Hirsch — *Middleground,* 1950
Sovereign Thoroughbreds — *Dark Star,* 1953
Miss Dana Goldsmith — *Determine,* 1954
Mr. and Mrs. Donald A. Fruehling — *Iron Liege,* 1957
Mr. Herbert I. Moelis — *Forward Pass,* 1968
Mr. Harley Clemmons — *Cannonade,* 1974
Mr. Jacinto Vasquez — *Foolish Pleasure,* 1975
Gov. Hugh Carey — *Seattle Slew,* 1977
Miss Monique Yazigi — *Affirmed,* 1978
Mr. Sanford Bryant — *Spectacular Bird,* 1979
Mr. James L. Kerr — *Genuine Risk,* 1980
Mr. John P. Campo — *Pleasant Colony,* 1981
Hon. Paul Tonko — *Gato Del Sol,* 1982
Mr. John P. Font — *Sunny's Halo,* 1983

We gratefully acknowledge and thank Phyllis George Brown and former Governor John Y. Brown; Frank Fox, Lynn Stone, President, Edgar Allen, Media Relations Director, and Mary Ann Cooper, Museum Curator, all of Churchill Downs; Dan Mangeot, Marcheta Sparrow, and Art Lander of the Kentucky Derby Festival; Kay Lowe and Lois Mateus of the Kentucky Department of Art; the Kentucky Library and Archives; William Anderson of the Jockey Club; the *Louisville-Courier Journal,* the *Lexington-Herald Reader,* John Lee of *Thoroughbred Magazine;* Beverly Poore, Joyce Bixon, Jean Brandon, and last, but not less, a special thanks to our editor, Ken Stuart.

CONTENTS

FOREWORD

In the spring of 1948, Calumet Farm was coming up to the Kentucky Derby with two exciting three-year-old colts, Citation, who won the Chesapeake Stakes at Havre de Grace, and Coaltown, who won the Blue Grass Stakes at Keeneland.

I had a great relationship with the late Ben Jones, who was head trainer for Calumet at that time. I'd ridden two Kentucky Derby winners for him (Lawrin in 1938 and Whirlaway in 1941) and we understood each other.

Actually, it was Ben Jones's son, Jimmy, who was training Citation and the Eastern Division of the stable, while Ben Jones had Coaltown and the Midwestern Division. I rode Citation to win the Chesapeake and was impressed with him. But Coaltown was also impressive in winning the Blue Grass under Newbold Leroy Pierson, and when I got to Kentucky, shortly before the Derby, all my hardboot friends were telling me that Coaltown was the better of the two and that I was on the wrong horse.

I'd done that number before. In 1942, while I was riding for Greentree Stable, I had my choice of Devil Diver and Shut Out for the Kentucky Derby. I chose Devil Diver and felt foolish when Shut Out won under Wayne Wright. Devil Diver eventually proved to be much the better horse of the two, but the consolation was long delayed.

I went to Ben Jones, probably the greatest trainer that ever lived. "Ben," I said, "I don't want to make a mistake. Tell me the truth. Am I on the right horse for the Derby?"

"Eddie," he said, "you've made no mistake."

That's a roundabout way for me to tell you that you've made no mistake in purchasing *Portraits in Roses*. Like Citation, it's a winner. It's a tapestry of Kentucky Derby history, from the first winner, the fabled Little Red Horse, Aristides, to Sunny's Halo, who won the 109th running on May 7, 1983.

They are all in *Portraits in Roses;* the mighty Hindoo (1881), one of the greatest horses of the nineteenth century; Regret (1915), the lovely filly who beat the colts and made the Derby a national institution; Black Gold (1924), perhaps the most colorful winner of all; War Admiral (1937), son of the mighty Man o' War; Whirlaway (1941), who turned in the greatest finish in Derby history to win by 8 lengths; Northern Dancer (1964), who brought pride to Canadian racing and breeding with his record-breaking victory; and those modern cracks Secretariat (1973), Seattle Slew (1977), Affirmed (1978), and Spectacular Bid (1979).

There is no race in the United States to compare with the Kentucky Derby for excitement and drama, and Beverley Bryant, a talented artist, has captured the scene with an innovative technique that enhances the glory of the times. I enjoyed it immensely and I'll bet you will too. *Portraits in Roses* is 4 to 5 with me.

Eddie Arcaro
Miami, Florida

NOTE FROM THE ARTIST

For portraits of horses from 1875 to approximately 1900 I had to rely on photographs of paintings done before photography existed or early photographs that were crudely touched-up. The paintings were in the elongated English style—the horses looked more like greyhounds—so I took the markings, head, expression, and general conformation and compressed the animal into a proportionate horse but maintained the old riding style and silks of the jockey and the tack of the period. The backgrounds are completely authentic as well.

The book is made up of three sections. The first thirty-five illustrations are done in antique tones—sepia, antique green, and old gold.

In the 1920s and 1930s I introduce color, gradually increasing it until by the 1950s the images are full-color. The first 99 pieces are done with oil wash (turpentine and oil paint used like watercolor), which is applied before the detail is put in in pencil. The paint goes on before the pencil.

The last section is the decade that starts with 1973 and Secretariat, and includes three Triple Crown champions, the filly Genuine Risk, plus several horses that came close to the "Triple." These are full-color oils on canvas.

PORTRAITS IN ROSES

ARISTIDES * May 17, 1875

Owner H. P. McGrath rests on the rail as Aristides and jockey Oliver Lewis go to the post. The original grandstand is in the background, with the clubhouse at the far left.

The first Kentucky Derby drew forty-two nominations and fifteen entries. The stakes were $50 from each entry with $1,000 added by the Louisville Racing Association, as it was then called. The trophy was a magnificent 300-ounce silver punch bowl valued at $1,000.

Ten thousand racing fans streamed out to Churchill Downs on this warm spring day. Many headed for the infield in horse-drawn wagons, buggies, carts, and carriages. The clubhouse was a different scene. Ladies were dressed fashionably in long organdy gowns, ten-button gloves, and large, elaborate hats. Bettors favored the traditional auction pools over the newly introduced pari-mutuel system from France, and bookies took bets as low as a nickel. Under the stands Negro mammies served fried fish and chicken while on the track fourteen of the fifteen jockeys going to the post were black.

The flag fell, the drum rolled, and they were off! Volcano took the lead, then eased back. McGrath's second horse, Chesapeake, broke last. At the half-mile pole McCreery led, but soon fell behind Aristides and Ten Broeck. Aristides held the lead at the mile and McGrath, seeing his Chesapeake out of the money, signaled jockey Oliver Lewis to take Aristides in for the win. Aristides won, with Volcano second and late charger Verdigris third. The time of 2:37¾ set an American record for three-year-olds, with 100 pounds up, over one and a half miles. The "Little Red Hoss," as McGrath referred to his fifteen-hands-high colt, had won $2,850 for him, a rich purse for the day.

Price McGrath was a noted horse breeder and had earned for himself a colorful reputation. He had heeded the call to "go west young man," then settled in New York where he operated a gambling house. Returning to Kentucky, he established McGrathiana Stud. His white mansion became famous for burgoo feasts (a local stew) and he frequently opened his doors to the public.

Vagrant, William Astor's brown gelding with Bobby Swim astride, takes the lead from Parole.
Two fashionably dressed ladies and a gentleman cheer their horse on.

The 6,000 people who made their way to Churchill Downs on May 15 anticipated a good time. It was a dry, sunny, perfect day. The men were most elegant in high glossy boots, white vests with cravats, and derbies. They escorted ladies in long gowns that swept the floor.

The Derby had attracted the attention of many Easterners. Congressman John T. Morrisey of New York reportedly had wagered $1,000 but would not reveal on which horse. It could have been Parole, owned by tobacco magnate Pierre Lorillard, who was the favorite. Another New Yorker, William Astor, had other ideas. He had arranged just two weeks prior to the Derby to buy Vagrant from his Lexington owner, T. J. Nichols. In the event Vagrant won, Nichols would get the purse in lieu of the purchase price, at $2,950, a far better deal for him.

Colonel H. B. Johnson, the Tennessee horseman who had started the field for the inaugural Derby, was there to repeat his performance. The drum rolled and Parole shot out to the lead. At the half-mile, Vagrant was second but by the three-eighths pole had nudged into the lead. Parole faded badly at the finish and it was Vagrant by 2 lengths over Creedmore with Harry Hill third.

Vagrant raced until the age of ten, netting his owner some $13,875, a vast amount for the times, yet the honest gelding and winner of the second running of the Kentucky Derby ended his life pulling a cart in the streets of Lexington.

Trainer Ed "Brown Dick" Brown faces us as Baden-Baden with young jockey Billy Walker gallops past.

Newspapers from the major cities of the East and Midwest covered the third running of the Kentucky Derby, an indication of its growing prominence. Louisville firms closed at 1:00 P.M. on Derby Day, as they still do. Among the crowd were Kentucky senator James Beck and Dame Helena Modjeska, who would soon star in the American premiere of Ibsen's *A Doll's House* in Louisville.

As a local orchestra struck up "Dixie," the favorites for the Kentucky Derby, Leonard and Vera Cruz, stepped onto the track. Leonard dominated at the start while Baden-Baden got away fifth but soon rushed Leonard and charged into the lead at the finish to win by 2 lengths.

Baden-Baden's jockey, Billy Walker, had ridden Ten Broeck, perhaps one of the greatest horses then running, for two long-distance records against time at the Louisville Jockey Club track prior to the Derby. The records stand today. And Baden-Baden's trainer, Ed Brown, a winning rider in his youth, enjoyed great success and respect in his career and would have been a winning Derby owner had he not sold the 1898 victor, Plaudit, to John Madden.

Immediately after the race, J. T. Williams, the owner of 4th place finisher, Vera Cruz, challenged Baden-Baden's owner, Dan Swigert, to a match race with an inviting $2,500 tag. Swigert sagely refused, saying he wouldn't tempt the gods twice.

Watching the finish from the old grandstand, Maj. Barak Thomas turns away as his horse, the favored Himyar, is outdistanced by Day Star. Carriages and mule-drawn trolleys surround the original judges' stand in the infield.

Policemen at the Association track on Derby Day, 1878, wore new summer uniforms and stiff-brimmed straw hats. Lemonade stands sprouted up in the infield, which was opened free to the public. The 6,000 fans took the opportunity to see firsthand the famous three-year-olds as well as politicians like Gen. Eli H. Murray, later governor of Utah, and famous minstrel and Baptist minister, Billy Emerson, who secretly bet the winner Day Star.

Maj. Barak Thomas, who owned the favorite, Himyar, was the sheriff of Fayette County, and a Confederate war veteran who'd returned to Kentucky to breed horses. He was an innovator in racing practices and initiated the use of numbers on saddlecloths. Fearing foul play the night before the Derby, he'd slept in Himyar's stall; however, he had to stand by helplessly on Derby Day as Himyar was bumped by every horse in the race. Day Star led from start to finish.

Day Star, bred by John Clay, son of Henry Clay, at Ashland, was purchased as a yearling for $825 by T. J. Nichols, the same T. J. Nichols who had sold the 1876 winner, Vagrant, two weeks before the Derby. Day Star's career really began in his third year with the Kentucky Derby, his first major win. A grandson of Lexington, he was the third Lexington descendant to win the Derby in its short four-year history. The chestnut colt ultimately raced a total of six years both on the flat and later over fences.

Jockey Charles Shauer on Lord Murphy, the first of three Tennessee-breds to win the Derby, poses in front of the original clubhouse built in 1875.

Louisville in 1879 was recovering from the financial panic that began in 1873. The return to prosperity was evident in the double-breasted jackets and Derby bowlers of the city's well-dressed men.

There was pari-mutuel wagering at the Louisville oval, but most bettors still favored auction pools that were sold at the Galt House in downtown Louisville. The fifth Kentucky Derby was to be a contest between horses from Tennessee and Kentucky. Kentucky breds had won the first four Derbies and were generally regarded as among the finest racehorses in the world. Lord Murphy, bred in Tennessee, was the favorite. Falsetto, bred in Frankfort, Kentucky, by Hunt Reynolds and ridden by Isaac Murphy, was the prime contender. Though he finished second, he later sired three Derby winners.

The drum rolled, the red bunting fell, and General Pike and Trinidad took the lead into the first turn. While pushing to the front, Lord Murphy was bumped and almost knocked out of the race. He recovered in time to charge from seventh in a field of nine and win by a length over Falsetto.

Lord Murphy was subsequently bought by Kentucky breeder James Keene and raced at America's best tracks for the remainder of his three-year-old year. At four and five the bay colt raced in England, but making only one start each year, he was unplaced in both races. Lord Murphy was the fourth of fifty-two Derby winners descended from the great sire, Lexington.

Robert A. Alexander, who bred Fonso, poses with the chestnut colt in front of his mansion at Woodburn Stud. He was the first man in the U.S. to make thoroughbred breeding a profession.

The sixth running of the Kentucky Derby was called the dust bowl by writers and racegoers who attended the event. The track was covered with dust several inches thick, making it nearly impossible for anyone to see the race—including the jockeys.

Alexander was a founding member of the Kentucky Association for the Improvement of the Breeds of Stock, which came into being when the Civil War changed the way of life in the South. The old genteel manner was gone, and the great thoroughbreds could no longer be raised for sport. The refinement of the racehorse became a business.

In the days Alexander held his sales at Woodburn, business was conducted in an atmosphere quite different from today's plush pavilions: the yearlings ran free until sales time. At the sales prospective buyers had to make themselves comfortable standing under the shade trees or sitting cross-legged on the grass.

J. S. Shawhan purchased Fonso as a yearling from Woodburn in 1878. The chestnut colt was a son of King Alfonso, the stud who replaced the great Lexington at Woodburn when he died there in 1875. Alexander had purchased Lexington for the sum of $15,000, the highest price paid up to that time for an American stallion.

One of a total of five Kentucky Derby winners produced by Woodburn, Fonso began his three-year-old career by winning the Phoenix Stakes at Lexington. His next start was the Derby, where he broke in front of the five-horse field and stayed in the lead the entire mile and a half to win over Kimball by 7 lengths. Kimball's rider, Billy Lakeland, claimed foul against Fonso, but it was disallowed. Fonso started only one more time as a three-year-old in the Viley Stakes and was second.

HINDOO * May 17, 1881

The great champion in his stall with the Dwyer Brothers and trainer James Rowe, Sr.

Fans flocked to Louisville in every manner of conveyance from cart to coach and tandem. The crowd filled the track grounds trying to get a glimpse of the renowned Hindoo, one of the greatest Derby champions of all times. He turned out to be a source of frustration to his owners, Philip and Michael Dwyer, who were betting men and could never get a decent price on their star performer. The Dwyers, two butchers from Brooklyn, made quite a contrast to the Wall Street types who filled the ranks of racehorse owners. A contemporary writer said: "It would not be accurate to say that the Dwyer Brothers dominated racing in their time, but they came near it. For thirty years there was hardly a great race run in which one of their horses did not figure conspicuously." Midway through a two-year-old season in which the bay colt won seven stakes, Hindoo was purchased by the brothers.

In the seventh Kentucky Derby, each of Hindoo's five challengers took a shot at him during the course of the mile and a half, but Hindoo withstood them all for an easy win. He was to go on to win 13 more stakes that year, one of them, the Monmouth Sweepstakes, an uncontested walkover. He lost his first race at four, but came back two days later to win at a mile and a quarter. Four days after that he scored at a mile and an eighth, then took a four-day breather again before tallying another win at a mile and a quarter.

His last start was the Coney Island Cup, a marathon two and a quarter miles. He won easily but broke down, finishing him as a racehorse. Consequently, the Dwyers stopped entering their horses in distance trials, leading the trend toward shorter races.

The starter cracked his whip and the horses were racing. Apollo, second from the outside, was on his way to victory in the eighth Kentucky Derby.

The Louisville Jockey Club had expanded the seating capacity of the track to nearly double its original size. The stands could now seat 42,000, more than any other track in the country. The Dwyer Brothers were confident of a win. Their horse Runnymeade was the favorite and Hindoo had won effortlessly for them the previous year.

Fate, however, smiled instead on Apollo's owners, Morris and Patton, and his breeder, Daniel Swigert, who had bred Hindoo. Apollo, the chestnut gelded son of Ashtead or Lever (the latter is given credit), had begun his career as a three-year-old. The grandson of Lexington took three major stakes races at three different tracks before going on to Louisville.

The horses now formed a ragged line across the track as was the system then. The drummer rolled his drum, the red flag fell. Runnymeade took command and looked the easy winner until jockey Babe Hurd started his charge on Apollo one-eighth mile from the finish. Apollo caught Runnymeade a few "jumps" from the imaginary line and won by a half-length.

Apollo finished his three-year-old year with 10 wins in 21 starts, then as a four-year-old went on to win 14 races, 9 of them in succession, out of 30 trips to the post.

In those early days a thoroughbred was raced and raced again unmercifully, sometimes twice in a week or every other day. In some instances, a horse was raced twice in the same day and over courses much longer than what the modern racegoer has come to expect. Long-distance trials of three and four miles were not uncommon. The thoroughbreds of the 1880s and 1890s were by necessity a stockier lot, heavier in body and legs that had to endure so much more concussion than our fine-legged speedsters of today. The early American racehorse rarely snapped a foreleg, suffered buck shins, or broke down.

Leonatus, son of Longfellow, poses with jockey Billy Donohue in the silks of co-owners Jack Chinn and G. W. Morgan. In the background a gentleman rests against his penny-farthing bicycle.

The Louisville Jockey Club Course, as it was then called, was rapidly becoming the best track in the country under the supervision of its creator, Col. M. Lewis Clark. Inspired by the 1872 Epsom Derby in England, Clark had formed the Louisville Jockey Club upon his return to the States and leased land for the track from relatives—John and Henry Churchill. With $100 from each of 320 original members, Clark built his track—a bargain at $32,000. It remained the Louisville Jockey Club Course or Louisville Race Track until 1886, when a columnist dubbed it "Churchill Downs" and the name stuck. Impartial, as a presiding judge, and always impeccably turned out, Colonel Clark presented an imposing figure complete with boutonniere and field glasses. A promoter first and a horseman second, he possessed only one white mare he used to pull his buggy.

Of fifty nominations for the Kentucky Derby, seven started in this its ninth running. Leonatus, the 9 to 5 favorite, paid $14.80 and took home $3,760. (Second place was a mere $200.)

Leonatus was beaten in his only race as a two-year-old. At three he was started at Lexington, Kentucky, where he won the Blue Ribbon Stakes. His next win would put him in the pages of history. In the Derby, Leonatus caught leader Drake Carter in the first quarter and never was headed, winning by 3 lengths. His three-year-old season was brilliant but his career short, as he broke down in training and never ran again. His phenomenal record of 10 wins and 1 second in 11 starts earned him $21,435, a large amount for the day, and a tidy profit for Messrs. Chinn and Morgan, who had paid a mere $5,000 for the bay colt. Leonatus's sire, Longfellow, fathered another Derby winner Riley (1890) before his death at Frank Harper's Natura Stud.

Buchanan, the winner of the tenth Kentucky Derby. Isaac Murphy, his celebrated black jockey, also rode winners Riley (1890) and Kingman (1891).

In 1884, Louisville suffered a flood so devastating the population gave up their buggies and carts for rowboats and canoes. The watery spring did not, however, deter the 5,000 enthusiasts who showed up at the Jockey Club Track for the tenth running of the "Big Race."

Buchanan was the first horse Isaac Murphy was to ride to victory in the Kentucky Derby. Murphy went on to be the first jockey to win two Derbies back to back and the first jockey voted to the American Racing Hall of Fame in the Racing Museum at Saratoga Springs, a record not matched for 39 years and not bested for 57 years. He was known for his pleasing personality and was completely honest, an attribute not possessed by all riders of his day or ours. By his own records, he rode 1,412 races in his career and won 628, or 44 percent. Eddie Arcaro, who rode five Derby winners himself and had a 20 percent winning average, said he doubted whether any jockey would ever come close to this.

Buchanan was temperamental and would just as soon throw a rider as carry him. Isaac Murphy had ridden him at Nashville where the colt had bolted and run off, and Murphy was not overjoyed at the prospect of riding him again. But the Jockey Club judges and Col. Clark threatened to penalize Murphy if he refused to ride.

Buchanan started badly and Bob Miles, followed by Powhattan III and the favorite, Audrain, took the lead. Murphy was undaunted. With the tenacity and courage that earned him lasting distinction, he managed to save ground on the first turn, pull ahead in the stretch, and win by 2 lengths. Isaac Murphy, known as the gentle jockey, never once used whip or spur.

Buchanan continued to race through 1886, earning a total of $13,110. His Derby win paid $20 for a $5 ticket—enough money in those preinflationary times to buy almost a month's worth of groceries.

Joe Cotton poses with a well-dressed young groom in front of a mule-drawn trolley, the main conveyance of the day.

Louisville was laying electric streetcar lines in 1885 that would in time provide direct transportation from downtown to the track. Cartoonist Fontaine Fox made the car famous as the "Toonerville Trolley" after it was electrified.

Joe Cotton, a chestnut son of King Alfonso, went off at even money having won six major stakes as a two-year-old and was heavily favored in the "tip" sheets. The betting guides first appeared at the Louisville Race Track in 1885 when a group of young boys offered them for sale. They proved amazingly accurate, and Joe Cotton was no exception. In seventh position, Joe Cotton made his move in the backstretch and slowly worked his way to the front. He had to be ridden to his ultimate effort to stave off the dual rush of Berson and Ten Booker, who came on like whirlwinds in the stretch.

Joe Cotton continued his winning ways, taking the largest purses in the Great Western Handicap, Coney Island Derby, Tidal Stakes, Himyar Stakes, and four others in his three-year-old season. He won four additional stakes before retirement after his sixth season and a total of $29,365 earned.

A. J. Alexander of Woodford County bred five Kentucky Derby winners of which Joe Cotton was the third, yet he never owned a Derby starter. He had taken over the breeding operation upon the death of his brother, Robert, who had saved it from marauding bands of guerrillas who laid waste to farms in the South during the Civil War. Robert, fearing the loss of his farm, had advertised his great sire, Lexington, and other stallions for sale. He gave thirty-four horses to Harry Belland to race and sell as he saw fit. Belland earned $300,000 in purses and sales in four years and saved Woodburn from disaster. Woodburn Stud went on to flourish under A. J.'s guidance.

BEN ALI * May 14, 1886

Owner James Ben Haggin studies the "card" as Ben Ali is cooled out. Two prosperous gentlemen look on in admiration in the casual setting of the times.

James Ben Haggin, a native Kentuckian who had made his fortune in copper and gold in California, had arrived in Louisville from the East only to find the "bookmakers" had gone on strike. Haggin informed the track officials that if no satisfactory settlement was found he would withdraw his considerable string of horses from the meeting. He let it be known in no uncertain terms that he wanted to back his own horses. The next day the bookies were on the track. However, a track official's derogatory remark was reported to him and he moved his horses out of Louisville the day after winning the Derby. It was a quarter of a century before Haggin returned to Kentucky and established Elmendorf Farm with its twenty-five rooms and impeccable lawns. The millions from his vast holdings enabled him to make Elmendorf one of the greatest blue grass estates of the era. He became the largest commer-cial breeder of thoroughbreds in the country. Named for his son, Ben Ali was Haggin's pride and joy. The colt was the son of Virgil, who had previouly sired the Derby winners Vagrant (1876) and Hindoo (1881).

Seven horses in the 1886 Derby field were Kentucky breds and all carried 118 pounds, the first time that weight had been assigned, with a 5-pound allowance for fillies. Ben Ali was favored. At the start, Masterpiece broke in front and was followed to the first turn by Harrodsburg and Sir Joseph. At the three-quarter-mile mark, Free Knight took the lead with "Snapper" Garrison in the irons, followed by Blue Wing and Ben Ali under Pat Duffy. Ben Ali and Blue Wing battled neck and neck through the stretch until Ben Ali pulled ahead to win by a half-length, setting a new Derby record. In his three-year-old campaign, Ben Ali took top honors in 7 of 12 starts.

Jockey Isaac Lewis sits astride Montrose. The bay colt was bred by Col. Milton Young, of Ohio, who purchased the famous McGrathiana Stud upon the death of Price McGrath. In the background, a mule-drawn water wagon wends its way up the dirt road.

James Ben Haggin, millionaire horseman and speculator, had withdrawn his stable from the last year's meeting a day after winning the Derby with Ben Ali. Haggin shunned Louisville, including the Derby, and raced instead in the East and in California. Without the Haggin entries, the field was one of the smallest ever started in a Kentucky Derby and judged by horsemen of the day as inferior to years past.

However, the crowd never weakened in enthusiasm. They were there for a good time and to be "on the winner." The stage was being set for the fashion shows of the future. The well-dressed man sported a straw Conductor, Breakman, or Buckner "boater," while the more affluent wore the world-renowned Knox.

As the seven candidates paraded before the stands, the favorite, Banburg, was wildly cheered. Montrose received only a polite reception, mostly by the Ohioans who had backed him. There were 119 nominations received for the thirteenth running of the classic race. Starter Billy Cheatham got the field away without incident. Jacobin led at the first but was soon overtaken by Montrose. The favorite challenged but Montrose outran him in the backstretch. Jim Gore moved up quickly in the final dash, but Montrose held on and won easily. The thirteenth Kentucky Derby winner was the second of the Matchem bloodline to triumph at the Derby after Baden-Baden (1877).

Macbeth II on the backstretch with young George Covington up. In the infield fans watch from a farm wagon and a mule-drawn streetcar, public transportation of the day.

Fourteen thousand fans braved a cold, windy day to see the Kentucky Derby. The favorite was Gallifet and coupled with Alexandria made up the entry from Melbourne Stable. But the brown gelding, Macbeth II, the son of Macduff, carrying the orange and black silks of the Chicago Stable, was about to take the silver punch bowl—the first time a Derby winner would carry a stable's colors. The year of 1888 was also the inaugural of the Belmont Futurity in New York, with its rich purse of $40,900.

As the horses lined up for the Derby a motion from the flagman sent them off early. The second start was clean and The Chevalier jumped into the lead. He was soon overtaken by Gallifet, who led the pack until well into the homestretch, when Macbeth II with young George Covington bolted to the front and took the race by a length.

The first race on the program this Derby Day had been a rerun. The horses had started from the half-mile pole instead of the intended five-eighths pole, and rather than postpone the race to a later date, the officials simply ran the tired horses again—this time an eighth of a mile longer!

Macbeth II won $22,170, and was the third gelding to win the Derby; not another would do so until Old Rosebud in 1914.

And no other Derby winner till then would go on to race as much as Macbeth II did in his lifetime—106 starts in seven seasons, of which 25 were wins.

A victory portrait of Spokane done in the style of the period.

The year 1889 saw the first $2 ticket sold, and it was also the last year auction pools would be allowed. They were discontinued until Churchill Downs president Matt Winn reinstated them in 1908. This was also the year Louisville got its first electric streetcar. The last mule-drawn trolley would leave the streets in 1901.

Sammy Barnes, the crack lightweight, was chosen to ride Proctor Knott, but Barnes was too small to control the big favorite. Spokane, bred in Illinois, foaled in Montana, and trained in Tennessee, had raced well as a two-year-old but not as well as Proctor Knott. A chestnut colt by Hyder Ali and a descendant of Lexington, Spokane's odds were 10 to 1. Proctor Knott broke away from the start twice, bolting each time a good eighth of a mile down the track. Nearly unseating his rider with a series of spectacular lunges, he nevertheless broke with the field on the third try and shot to an early lead, which he opened to five lengths as they rounded the clubhouse turn. Entering the far turn, jockey Tom Kiley sent Spokane skimming along the rail past Once Again and pulled almost even with Proctor Knott with a quarter mile left to run. It became a desperate match race: at the one-eighth pole, just when he appeared to have it won, Proctor Knott bolted for the outer rail, and by the time "Pike" Barnes had straightened his colt, Spokane had gained a slim lead, which he managed to hold despite Proctor Knott's last desperate drive.

The margin of victory was a nose, and the crowd remained convinced that Proctor Knott was the better horse, with the exception of Frank James, Jesse's brother, who had $5,000 on Spokane. A few days later, Spokane came back to prove his class with another game score over his highly touted rival in the Clark Stakes at one and one-quarter miles.

Owner-trainer "Big Ed" Corrigan proudly leads his winner with jockey Isaac Murphy before an admiring group including jockey Billy Lakeland. The ornate original grandstand is in the background with its single spire and twin towers.

A downpour kept the crowd on the small side at the sixteenth Derby, even though the city had closed the pool halls for the duration of the meet to encourage track attendance. Six starters faced the flag, one of the smallest fields to date, with Robespierre going off as the even money favorite. That colt put on a wild display parading to the post, convincing even more bettors that this was the beast to back. The start was good and the horses stayed tightly bunched as they passed the stands for the first time. Riley trailed the pack. Halfway down the backstretch Isaac Murphy gave Riley his head, and as they entered the far turn, Riley was in front by 2 lengths, an advantage he maintained at the wire. He became the winner of the first of many rain-soaked Derbies.

Riley, a bay colt by Longfellow, was the second of three Derby winners for Isaac Murphy, the jockey who many believed had a special communication with horses. Murphy would win the Derby the following year on Kingman, and Riley's sire, Longfellow, had already produced the 1883 Derby winner, Leonatus—whose victory had also come over a wet track.

A few days later, as trainers thought nothing then of running a horse twice in one week, Riley was back on the track for the Clark Stakes, which he also won. Of his 64 career starts, Riley won 30, and despite starting 21 times in his three-year-old year and 15 in his four-year-old year, continued to race without breaking down until his retirement in 1894, his seventh year. His career earnings total was $43,430.

KINGMAN * May 13, 1891

Isaac Murphy on Kingman in the winner's circle with Jacobin Stable co-owner Kinzea Stone.

Louisville's Union Station was completed in 1891. For the next fifty years the station would be a famous meeting place for arriving Derby guests.

On that second Saturday in May, the infield was so congested that the starter needed a police escort to clear a path to the half-mile pole where the mile-and-a-half classic would begin. "Ike" Murphy rode Kingman, who ran the slowest Derby before or since. Without each other's knowledge, the owners and trainers of each of the four-horse field—one of the smallest in Derby history—instructed their riders to lay back for most of the race, then charge at the finish. A quarter mile from home all four were across the track, nose to nose, as if in a cavalry charge. Then Balgowan made his move and Murphy took off after him. Kingman won by a half-length.

Kingman had been bred in Tennessee by A. C. Franklin and was the second Derby winner to hail from that state, the first being Lord Murphy in 1879. The brown colt raced only two years, earning nearly $20,000 in 28 starts, a large amount for the day.

Kingman was Isaac Murphy's third Derby victory. He'd begun his riding career in 1874, a year before the first Kentucky Derby, at the age of fourteen. He weighed only 70 pounds and went to work for the stable of Williams and Owings. At the time many of the jockeys were black, as they were the only ones who handled the horses and knew and rode them best. Fifteen of the first twenty-eight Derbies were won by black jockeys. As the sport became more lucrative, white jockeys took over.

Just prior to his death in 1896, Murphy was quoted as saying, "I am as proud of my calling as I am of my record, and I believe my life will be recorded as a success, though the reputation I enjoy was earned in the stable and the saddle."

Azra, the bay colt with young jockey Alonzo Clayton catches Huron at the wire in the 18th running.
The original judges' stand is in the background.

The 1892 Kentucky Derby with only three starters was the smallest field to date. Originally, owner George Long—also the breeder of Derby winners Manuel (1899) and Sir Huon (1906)—planned to have stablemate Bashford run with Azra, however, when rain left the course heavy, trainer John Morris decided to scratch Bashford. The two horses had raced brilliantly during 1891 and were considered the best two-year-olds of that season.

Jockey Britton on Huron tried to set a pace that would kill Azra and Phil Dwyer. Swinging the big bay colt to the rail, he drew away from Azra, who Clayton held well in hand, and gradually increased his lead by 5 lengths. Phil Dwyer was held in reserve by jockey Overton. Nearing the first quarter they all ran wide at the turn seeking drier ground. Down the backstretch, Huron ran easily 2 lengths in the lead. Huron looked like the winner as the crowd cheered. As they neared the last quarter, Azra gained on Huron, forging to the front. They reached the stretch on even terms. The stands swelled with excitement. By the eighth pole, Huron had pulled a neck ahead of Azra, but as they approached the finish Azra made another rush and caught Huron to win by a nose. The 10,000 in attendance witnessed this fine test of courage and cheered winner and loser alike.

Following his Derby triumph, Azra won the Clark Stakes and left Churchill Downs for the East, where he won the Travers Stakes at Saratoga and placed frequently in other races. Although successful, Azra's career was woefully short: one morning, when trainer Morris had invited a number of friends to the barn to inspect his string and Azra had been paraded for the guests, his groom rushed back to Morris with the news that the great horse was "down" in his stall. The winner of the 1892 Kentucky Derby was dead at the age of three.

Described in a Louisville paper a day after his win as splendidly muscled with a better set of legs seldom placed under a thoroughbred, the rich golden chestnut poses with his groom. Trainer William McDaniel is in the background.

Drenched by rain the day and night before, the track was wet but fast by race time. The sun came out in the morning and 30,000 racing enthusiasts headed for the "Downs." This year for the first time women were allowed to place their own wagers.

More horses had shown up for this meeting than any other in the track's history, and temporary stabling had been set up in an old hay barn and every other available shed as they poured in by the train carload from as far away as Washington, D.C. "Railbirds" were in despair. Although they'd been able to clock the final pre-Derby workouts of nearly all the entries, Plutus had eluded them and it was confusing their bookmaking. If trainer Morris had given the Bashford Manor colt a final breeze it must have been in the dark.

Among the entries, there were three outstanding horses that had done well on a wet track: Boundless in the Arkansas Derby, Lookout at Memphis, and Linger in the Distillers Stakes at Lexington. In addition, Buck McCann would benefit from his sire's talent for the slop, his sire having been the 1884 winner, Buchanan.

Lookout's jockey, Ed Kunze, had received his instructions from trainer William McDaniel to "kill 'em," and from the time the crimson bunting fell, Lookout dominated. With not a spot of mud on his golden coat, he galloped past the finish pole untouched by steel or whip, leaving in his wake 4 lengths back the five weary stragglers. It had been a fine field, with each horse worthy of a Derby appearance, but they'd been made to look unfit by the excellence of Lookout. It had been a June day in 1886 when Troubadour, Lookout's sire, had triumphed in much the same way at the Sheepshead Bay Racecourse.

Trainer Eugene Leigh tacks up the eventual winner as jockey Frank Goodale looks on in controlled anticipation.

In 1894 a twenty-four-year-old native Louisvillian, Joseph D. Valdez, saw what would be his most famous architectural creation erected at Churchill Downs. The new grandstand with its twin spires would face the east, a welcome improvement for racegoers, who formerly had to stare into the sun throughout an afternoon's racing.

Small fields had plagued the Derby since Haggin had walked out with his string of top horses after his 1886 Derby win with Ben Ali. Many Eastern stables had boycotted the Downs in sympathy. Also, as racing had become increasingly more a business than a sport, owners were reluctant to run their best colts the grueling one-and-a-half-mile distance so early in the season. These factors, plus the financial instability of the track, contributed to the lightness of the field—only five started. By the end of the year the Clark regime had fallen, replaced by the New Louisville Jockey Club, which put $100,000 into track improvements, including the new grandstand; however, the current Derby distance of one-and-a-quarter miles would not be instituted until 1896.

Despite the perfect weather and record crowd, the twentieth Kentucky Derby was not one of the most memorable. All five starters carried the same impost—122 pounds—perhaps one cause for the unspectacular event. The winner was decided before the race was half over. Chant led at the half-mile by 2 lengths and loped past the wire with the field strung out for 40 lengths behind him. With a time of 2:41, it was the slowest Derby with the exception of Riley in 1890. The fastest had been Lord Murphy in 1879.

Fate had smiled on jockey Goodale by giving him the most satisfying win a jockey could earn, only to take him from the track forever in a race two days after his Derby triumph. Goodale was killed in the saddle when his mount stumbled and fell.

Jockey James "Soup" Perkins steadies Halma. Perkins in Byron McClelland's silks (lower left, inset).

In the last three Derbies, a total of only fourteen horses had gone to the post and the track was losing money. Colonel Clark's Louisville Jockey Club had given way to the New Louisville Jockey Club, a group of professional gamblers. They realized that some drastic improvements had to be made and had funded the new grandstand and many other refurbishments. Unfortunately, the Derby distance of one-and-a-half-miles was not shortened.

The unpopular distance resulted in only four starters for the twenty-first Derby: Halma, with Perkins; Basso, with Martin; Laureate, with Clayton; and Curator, with Overton. Despite the small field, the opening of the new track was a huge success, drawing over 20,000.

Halma had the striking attributes of his sire, Hanover, the massive shoulder and perfect legs, deep chest and flowing action. A cheer swelled from the crowd as the sixteen-year-old "Soup" Perkins, in McClelland's green and orange colors, rode from the paddock.

The track was fast and the race was decided early. Little "Soup" had wrapped the reins around his arms up to his elbows hoping to hold Halma, who charged to the front in spite of him and pulled away from the field. As they neared the grandstand for the first time he had opened his lead to a length. Laureate held on, but Curator "stopped" with comical quickness. Halma widened his lead to 2 lengths at the mile, and still under Soup's tight wraps, appeared to be out for an exercise gallop. He romped under the wire 3 lengths ahead of his nearest pursuer.

James Perkins was the youngest jockey to win the Derby, a record unbroken until Steve Cauthen on Affirmed in 1978. The year of Halma's Derby saw the retirement of the great Isaac Murphy, known to all as Honest Ike.

BEN BRUSH * May 6, 1896

Ben Brush breathes heavily as jockey Willie Simms unsaddles him after their victory in the twenty-second Derby.

It was the beginning of a new era. Declaring the mile-and-a-half distance too grueling a test, the new management shortened the race to a mile and a quarter, which it is today. The new length was an immediate success with the horsemen as a record 171 horses were nominated that year, although only 8 started. Among the entrants was the Eastern "Wonder Horse," Ben Brush, making a rare Southern appearance.

At the start, Semper Ego and Ben Brush took an early lead. Then Ben Brush stumbled but recovered, and going into the turn past the stands the horses were tightly bunched. Suddenly, like a thunderbolt, First Mate broke from the pack and was 2 lengths on top by the backstretch with the favorite, Ben Brush, coasting in fourth place. Ben Brush made his move along with Ben Eder, and by the top of the stretch it was a four-horse race with First Mate losing ground and Semper Ego straining to keep pace. With Ben Eder on his flank, Willie Simms called on Ben Brush for everything he had. The bay colt started to weaken, but Simms dug in his spurs and they reached the finish nose to nose, the big Eastern horse the winner by inches. It was a thrilling Derby. Ben Brush triumphed but many considered Ben Eder the better horse.

Ben Brush was the leading sire of 1909 when his sons and daughters accumulated $75,143 in purse money. His great-granddaughters produced Derby winners Bubbling Over, War Admiral, and Whirlaway. Of his sons, Broomstick sired Meridian (1911 Derby) and Regret, the first filly to take the honors in 1915.

The untimely death of the great jockey Isaac Murphy one year after his retirement shocked the racing world of 1896. Over 500 people, as many black as white, attended his funeral. The $30,000 he left to his wife was decimated by debts and she died childless in a pauper's grave. Only a simple wooden cross marked his grave which was soon obscured by weeds and grass. It was eventually discovered and Murphy's remains were moved to a Lexington park where he was reburied near the grave of Man o' War.

Isaac Murphy had fallen victim to the rigors of losing up to 40 pounds each time racing season came around, compounded by doses of champagne he drank to keep going. His resistance at an all-time low, he died of pneumonia at the age of thirty-five.

The drummer has rolled his drum, the starter's gun has gone off, and the assistant starters slash at the field with their whips.

Most of the smart money had been on the favorite, Ornament, in the pools that were still operated in downtown Louisville, despite much grumbling from the bookmakers. As the drizzle started Tuesday morning, however, those in the Typhoon II camp took heart as he had proven to have a liking for the slop. "Buttons" Garner, Fred Taral's replacement on Typhoon II, was so confident that he had advised his cohorts to put their money on his horse.

Twenty thousand were treated to a contest that was in doubt up until the end. Typhoon II, bred and owned in the sister state of Tennessee, had plunged and wheeled and after "only" 6 minutes at the start, took the lead immediately. Left at the post and caught in the heavy going, Ornament gamely tried to close in on the leader, who led from pole to pole with such a burst of speed that not one of the nation's best three-year-olds could catch the chestnut colt. Ornament ran a suspiciously timed race. He came flying from behind but could do no better than reach Typhoon II's saddlecloth in a last desperate surge at the finish line.

Charlie Patterson, the trainer and part-owner of Ornament, was found later in his barn whittling casually on a railing as his horse was cooled out. Apparently unperturbed by the upset, he allowed as how it had happened before and probably would again. But "Buttons" Garner was jubilant. Taking great whiffs of his roses between short breaths as he stepped off the scales, he said he had known no horse could touch them except Ornament and that when Alonzo Clayton had finally set sail for Typhoon, at the final eighth, "Buttons" had simply to lean forward a little and speak to his horse.

In the paddock, Plaudit's owner, John Madden (in straw hat), plans strategy with jockey Willie Simms.

The morning of the Derby had been wet and gloomy and the expected record crowd never materialized despite clearing skies in the afternoon. Plaudit, a son of Himyar, who had been deprived of victory twenty years earlier by Day Star and a plot to defeat him, would this day vindicate his sire's loss. The Kentucky Derby was the brown colt's first start as a three-year-old. His owner-trainer, John Madden, would be America's leading breeder from 1912 until 1927 and the first breeder to produce a Triple Crown winner (Sir Barton), yet no victor in the Derby would ever carry his colors after Plaudit.

The race was a masterpiece of riding by jockey Willie Simms. When the flag fell, Lieber Karl shot to the front with Han d'Or and Isabey in hot pursuit.

Plaudit was last, running easily. On the backstretch, he moved on Lieber Karl leaving Han d'Or and Isabey in the dust. At the top of the stretch, Plaudit caught Lieber Karl. Plaudit kept stride with the big colt and moved to take over the lead in the stretch. The crowd went wild as both horses fought a desperate duel for a short distance. Then Plaudit was in front, gradually drawing away, and crossed the finish first by a neck.

It was the second Derby win in three years for Willie Simms. Simms was the first jockey ever to ride "short" although that credit has been awarded to the English jockey Tod Sloan. Actually, Simms rode short in that country one year before Sloan.

Although the upright style of the jockeys makes them appear to be out for a canter, this is a hard-fought battle with Manuel and Fred Taral (insert) besting His Lordship at the top of the stretch.

Starting with Manuel in 1899 and ending with Donerail in 1913, the Derby was characterized by mediocrity. The trend started with Typhoon II's win in 1897 when the favorite, Ornament, received a suspicious ride, and coupled with the change in management and local opposition to gambling the Derby became a local affair riding on its reputation. Col. M. Lewis Clark, the father of Churchill Downs and the Derby, sadly ended his life by his own hand two weeks before the twenty-fifth running.

Since the Derby's inception in 1875, 24 winners and over 180 hopeful three-year-olds had passed under the wire. And though the year's entries were slim (only five horses paraded to the post), the crowd was large and the racing of high quality. True to form, Manuel sprang to the front as the bunting fell. Jockey Fred Taral, saving the bay colt, pulled back behind His Lordship and Fontainebleu, and as the field passed the stands for the first time, Taral had Manuel comfortably in third place. Keeping his mount within striking distance, Taral waited for the right moment and sent him at the half mile. Manuel shot to the lead and was an easy victor by the homestretch. He crossed the finish a full 2 lengths to the good of Corsini. Corsini, tired from his long trip from the Pacific Coast, responded gamely to Burns's whip but couldn't catch the Dutchman from New York, who spurred Manuel on to insure his win. Manuel was never fully extended.

Though a day of triumph for Manuel, many favorite sons mourned the passing of Colonel Clark and reflected on the good old days of the Louisville Jockey Club when Clark ruled with an iron fist. Not only had he been an accomplished organizer and leader, but a respected track judge as well. Fair to a fault, no discrepancy eluded his attention and no favors were granted.

*Jockey Jimmy Boland casually poses with Lieutenant Gibson in front of Churchill Downs president
W. F. Schulte's coach-and-four.*

The air was clear and the track fast—a perfect day for the swiftest Derby ever. The twenty-sixth Derby was contested before a record crowd of 30,000 with a larger field than recent years.

An experimental rubber barrier snapped against the infield rail and a massive roar went up from the crowd as the race started. Lieut. Gibson broke with His Excellency and Kentucky Farmer. The three horses ran as if chained together and created a classic picture for the tabloids as they charged past the stands through a cloud of dust. At the first turn the race took on a different look with Lieut. Gibson first and the rest of the field second. Almost without effort Lieut. Gibson had swept into the lead he never relinquished. It was

reported that the great colt never extended himself yet bested Ben Brush's time for the inaugural run (1896) over the one and a quarter miles by 1⅖ seconds. Champion three-year-olds all, the balance of the field had been made to look like a bunch of "platers." Lieut. Gibson's record would stand for eleven years when Meridian would cover the distance in 2:05. Charles Head Smith, Lieutenant Gibson's owner, didn't have a dime on his horse, yet was pleased with the win not only for himself but for the entire Board of Trade of Chicago, who put a considerable amount of dimes on Lieutenant Gibson.

It was preferable to have your horse finish in the clear in those days, as the dust was so thick a close finish was nearly unjudgeable.

HIS EMINENCE   *   April 29, 1901

As though taking his cue from owner F. B. VanMeter, standing next to the latest in "two-wheelers,"
His Eminence strikes a formal pose.

Despite record crowds for the twenty-seventh Derby and a Derby record set the year before, the event was still in danger for its life. The great Eastern stables continued to shun it, and the Downs was still plagued by internal management problems and financial difficulties.

Another small field, but five of the country's best, went to the post, including His Eminence, with Jimmy Winkfield making his second Derby appearance (third the year before on Thrive) and jockey Jim Boland, the 1901 winner, on Driscoll. Sannazarro, billed earlier as the dark horse, would go off at better odds of 4 to 1. Alard Scheck was favored at 7 to 10. The top three horses had all worked speedily during their pre-Derby "blowouts" before an early morning crowd of 500, who saw His Eminence turn in the best time. The track was in its fastest condition ever and many expected records to be shattered left and right. The evening before the race, Jimmy Boland took himself out for a run with pugilist Jack McClelland in the hopes of shedding extra poundage, yet returned still 3½ pounds overweight, which may have figured in the results.

"They're off!" and before 50 yards had slid under his hooves, His Eminence had taken over the lead. Winkfield was riding beautifully as he passed the half-mile in :51. He had the race won and he knew it. Meanwhile, Alard Scheck, the odds-on favorite, was bringing up the rear. As His Eminence crossed the wire, Alard Scheck committed a racing sin. Instead of responding to his rider's urgings, he sulked and finished 5 lengths behind the last horse. Jimmy Boland on Driscoll finished third. This was the first of two winning performances in the saddle over a Derby course for black jockey Jimmy Winkfield. The next would come with Alan-a-Dale the following year.

32

ALAN-A-DALE * May 3, 1902

Jimmy Winkfield, dapper in sportcoat, slacks, and cap, gives Alan-a-Dale a pre-Derby workout.
Soulful and proud, he stares out at us from the past (inset).

The first automobile coughed down the boulevard and the electrification of the city's mule-cars was completed. Churchill Downs, however, was not prospering. The Derby was still drawing only average-size fields. Later in the year, Col. Matt Winn, a Louisville tailor with no horseracing experience, would form a group of buyers to take over the financially ailing track for a mere $40,000.

Alan-a-Dale, a chestnut son of Halma, the 1895 winner, was owned by Maj. T. C. McDowell, a great-grandson of Henry Clay, Kentucky's most popular statesman. He bred and trained the winner and was the only man to accomplish this beside T. P. Hayes with his Donerail in 1913.

The second jockey to win two Derbies back to back after Murphy, Winkfield had made his riding debut in Chicago in a rather spectacular fashion. Breaking on the outside, he cut off three horses in his rush to the inside rail and all four went down. Winkfield was ruled off for a year only to win his first time back. He holds the best winning average for the Derby—two wins, one second, and a third in only four attempts.

He rode one of his best races ever on Alan-a-Dale. McDowell had given jockey Nat Turner first choice of his two Derby hopefuls and Winkfield, who exercised them both and knew that Alan-a-Dale was the faster, held that horse back in workouts prior to Turner's visit. Turner picked The Rival. Alan-a-Dale, however, was so "bad-legged" he had to be trained in a driving cart.

The Rival was first to take the lead but soon surrendered it to Alan-a-Dale in the first eighth. Alan-a-Dale opened his lead to 4 lengths but going into the homestretch, went noticeably lame. As he started to bobble, Winkfield held him together and at the same time pushed Inventor, who had come up on the outside, farther out into the deep sand. Alan-a-Dale won by a nose. This was the first start as a three-year-old for this game young horse and one that cost him dearly. He did not start again until his fourth season.

Triple portrait of Trainer J. P. Mayberry and jockey Hal Booker in front of Judge Himes.

Early was the crowd's favorite. They could be forgiven for overlooking Judge Himes. He had managed to get to the wire first in only one of his 10 starts as a two-year-old, and failed to impress at three. But the chestnut colt was brought up to the classic by J. P. Mayberry, a trainer whose horses made up in conditioning what they lacked in class. Actually, Judge Himes should have looked like a good bet. He was owned by Charles R. Ellison, the "Blond Plunger," known to be one of the heaviest bettors in the country.

As it turned out, Judge Himes may have owed his win to a jockey—not his own, Hal Booker, but Jimmy Winkfield on the favorite, Early. Winkfield, having won the last two Derbies, had set his sights on beating Isaac Murphy's record of 3 wins with 2 back to back. Winkfield wanted 3 back to back. In his eagerness, he urged Early to run too soon, and when the sore-heeled Judge Himes came up on the inside, Early had nothing left.

Winkfield never forgot his faux pas. In telling the story later at his training stable in Maisons-Lafitte, France, he admitted he thought of fouling Judge Himes a little. He was a big favorite and probably would not have been disqualified. This opportunistic attitude got him in a bit of trouble with John Madden, which was one of the reasons that Wink ended up riding in Russia. "I was tops in Russia," he said.

*Frankie Prior on Elwood after his win is recorded for posterity by early movie cameras, which
filmed the Derby for newsreels that played turn-of-the-century movie houses.*

In 1904, Elwood's sire was earning his oats pulling a plow—one indication why Elwood's victory came at the longest odds to date. Being a Missouri bred didn't endear him to the bettors at the thirtieth running either.

The bay colt's record as a two-year-old was dreadful but he had put in a few fair tries at three, including a second in the California Derby. After arriving in Louisville, he was honed to razor sharpness by C. E. Durnell, husband of the horse's owner. Elwood was not only the first Derby winner owned by a woman, but he was the first bred by a woman, Mrs. J. B. Prather.

In the Derby, Elwood was piloted by Frankie Prior, a California farm boy. He was unknown in Louisville but had performed impressively on the West Coast. Prior rated his homely colt patiently as the small field of five moved through the first mile. With a quarter of a mile to go he was still dead last. Then Prior "got after" Elwood and they glided by the fading pacesetter with ease, arriving at the wire a half-length ahead of the favorite, Ed Tierney. This Derby win was to be the highlight of the Missouri invader's career. His only victory at four came in a curiosity event at New York's Brighton Beach Racetrack—a race restricted to jockeys who had never won.

C. E. "Boots" Durnell was not present when Elwood took the roses. He had not wanted to run the horse, thinking he hadn't a prayer of winning. His wife, the owner, disagreed and, when she won the argument, Durnell boycotted the whole affair and another trainer was asked to saddle Elwood in the paddock at Churchill Downs.

Trainer Robert Tucker holds Agile as jockey Jack Martin loosens his girth after the 31st Kentucky Derby. The new stands and clubhouse turn are on the right. The old bandshell where summer evening concerts were held is on the left.

S. Brown, Agile's owner, maintained a steel mill in Pittsburgh and a fleet of riverboats, which were used to haul coal and ore to it. As the operator of this fleet he dubbed himself "Captain."

Robert Tucker, as well known for his squinty eyes and handlebar moustache as for his talent as a trainer, was at the zenith of his career in 1905. The delicate-featured Jack Martin was a tough and clever jockey despite his "pretty boy" looks.

Nobody was out of the money in the 1905 Derby because only three horses had entered the contest. It was the smallest field ever with the exception of Azra's race in 1892. The competition was really only between Agile and Ram's Horn. Agile, the son of Sir Dixon and Alpena, was given the unbelievably short odds of 33¢ on the dollar.

The bugle called the three contenders from the paddock. As if he knew he were the favorite and sure winner, Agile shot under the flying web barrier and took the lead immediately. He never relinquished it, despite a bid in the stretch from Ram's Horn, and galloped under the wire. Jack Martin later stated that his horse would have won even if the track were powder-dry and not the heavy going of this race. Lucien Lyne, Ram's Horn's jockey, agreed. D. Austin, who rode Layson and finished 20 lengths behind Ram's Horn, refused to talk. As they passed the finish Martin was restraining Agile.

Sir Huon with jockey Roscoe Troxler painted in the English style of the period. A pair of grays pulled a gentleman's daycart toward the Derby champion.

The thirty-second running of the Louisville classic shaped up as a battle of the sexes. Sir Huon won this scrimmage, outlasting the game filly, Lady Navarre. The concensus of the day was that, game though she was, a filly just could not stand up to the rigors of the Derby.

Sir Huon had been bred in the Bluegrass State by George J. Long, an industrialist and sportsman who disliked commercialism, and believed in sport for sport's sake. Further, the Kentucky Derby was in Sir Huon's blood—he was the third winner sired by Falsetto. Chant and His Eminence preceded him. Sir Huon won 4 out of 9 starts in his first year, but came up to the Derby without a prep race. The results proved he didn't need it.

Superstition was the villain that caused Sir Huon to go off at overwhelming odds in his favor. The local paper had run a pre-Derby story with a picture that showed a number 5 horse clearly visible. That was Sir Huon's number and he evidently picked up a good deal of "action" from the hunch players. Laying second in the early going, he got a neck in front at the mile pole and stretched his advantage to 2 lengths at the wire. Lady Navarre overcame interference and fought valiantly in the stretch but could not get any closer to him. Jockey Roscoe Troxler said, "I felt confident of winning. I could feel the big colt was full of run under me." He claimed that toward the end, Sir Huon was only cantering. Lady Navarre's defeat would be vindicated in 1915 when Harry Payne Whitney's filly, Regret, would be the first horse of the feminine gender to wear the blanket of roses.

PINK STAR * May 6, 1907

Andy Minder has removed his boots and saddle to pose bareback on the bald-faced Pink Star.

Mrs. Nicholas Longworth, the former Alice Roosevelt, was the center of attraction at this thirty-third running—until the horses stepped onto the mud-spattered track. Then all those crowding in the stands and those watching from treetops on the "outside" strained to see the field. Tom Hayes's colt, Red Gauntlet, was the overwhelming favorite with odds of 3 to 2 over Ovelando at 3 to 1 odds, but Pink Star's owner, J. Hal Woodford from Versailles, Kentucky, remained confident. He'd seen his horse lose a race or two, yet sensed that Pink Star had enough strength in reserve to pull this one out of the hat.

As noted by the few who bet on him at 15 to 1, Pink Star was the very image of his sire, Pink Coat, who set the record for seven-eighths of a mile at Churchill Downs in 1900. Pink Star was also the grandson of the 1883 winner, Leonatus, and could trace his lineage back to Leamington, who sired the first Kentucky Derby winner, Aristides.

Jockey Minder rode an intelligent race, restraining the fleet bay colt in the early stages. He trailed far back for the first three-quarters and, gradually moving up through the far turn, straightened out for the stretch and came on with a rush that wore the leaders down. He won "going away." Little "Andy" Minder, whose career had been marred by bad luck and an injury at Churchill Downs, was the happiest boy in the world when owner Woodford gave him $500 for his great ride, performed down to the letter of Woodford's instructions.

Trainer J. W. Hall poses stoically with Arthur Pickens on Stone Street for their victory portrait with the rose blanket. "Movietone News" cameras recorded the event.

Col. Matt J. Winn, the chairman of Churchill Downs, got the bad news a few days before the Derby was to be run: bookmaking was made illegal and that law was to be enforced at Churchill Downs beginning with its Spring opener, the Derby of 1908. But the crafty colonel recalled the old pari-mutuel machines used at the track back in the 1880s. There were still a few gathering dust in storage that were serviceable, and through a flurry of telegrams he located a few more from as far away as New York. So that year, instead of bookmakers in the betting shed, there were eleven pari-mutuel machines, seven for win bets and two each for place and show.

Both bettors and the machine operators were unfamiliar with the new system, which created long, slow-moving lines. Many bettors found that they actually bought place or show tickets when they had wanted to back a winner on the nose. Some profited from their mistakes, but not if they had wanted to bet Stone Street to win. He paid $123.60 for every $5.00 bet.

The long shot had not been impressive coming up to the Derby, but on Derby Day the track came up heavy with mud. Stone Street's only decent race had been over that kind of track. Nineteen-year-old jockey Arthur Pickens felt the race was his when he found himself in second place after the first quarter-mile. At the top of the stretch Stone Street had a neck in front, increasing the margin to 3 lengths at the finish.

The Kentucky Derby was Stone Street's first, last, and only stakes win, and, at 2:15⅓, the slowest Derby ever run at one-and-a-quarter-miles. Kingman recorded the slowest over the one-and-a-half-mile-long course with a time of 2:52¼ in 1891.

Vincent Powers exercises Wintergreen under the admiring gaze of a group of dandies of the period. Note the "modern" stirrup length.

Politician-turfman J. B. "Rome" Respess, who owned Wintergreen, had generously contributed to various racetracks and desired his crowning gift to be a Derby winner. He spared no expense on his beautiful bay colt by Dick Welles. When Wintergreen was only a few weeks old, Respess had prophesied, "This one will be the winner of the Derby in 1909," and he did all that was necessary to achieve that end.

Although his only stakes placing up to the Derby was a meagre third in the Hurricane Stakes, Wintergreen had won 5 of his starts as a two-year-old, and had the additional advantage of guidance from a leading jockey of the day, Vincent Powers, who would later succeed as a trainer as well. Miami, a strong but unpredictable colt, simply could not compete with the popular favorite, though some doubted Wintergreen could go the distance and expected him to falter near the end. They were unaware that the blood of the great sires Virgil and Herod would help him stay the course.

It had rained the morning of the thirty-fifth running, but the track was in good shape. Going off at $1.96 to the dollar, Wintergreen was the obvious winner right from the start, where he was bumped by Dr. Barkley, but recovered instantly and took the lead. Then, the race well in hand with Miami hanging on behind him, Wintergreen faltered at the eighth pole. A muffled sigh went up from the crowd. Vincent Powers lashed at the handsome colt mercilessly, and he leaped ahead like a wounded deer and came on through the corridor of sound, past the forest of waving canes and umbrellas and the thousands cheering his name to the wire.

An historical montage: Robert Herbert poses bareback and awkwardly clutches his bouquet of roses astride the 1910 winner, Donau. In the background, the first plane to fly in the state of Kentucky prepares for takeoff from the infield at Churchill Downs.

Admission to the infield at the Downs was free in 1910's running, and thousands poured in from every state. The announcer's voice, amplified by a primitive microphone, was barely audible above the roar of the crowd, and there was some confusion as to which horse had drawn what track position.

Donau's owner, William Gerst, was one of 20 million immigrants who had come to "the land of milk and honey" since 1821. He had spent his childhood in Germany and built a lucrative brewery business in the United States. The name, Donau, means Danube in German.

Donau, whose short odds in this race were 1.65 to the dollar, raced more times than any other Derby winner. He had won 5 of his 10 outings as a two-year-old and eventually won 30 of his 111 starts in a four-year career. When the barrier flew up and the assistant starters' whips cracked like rifle fire, Donau went to the lead immediately and held on to it until the stretch, where he tired but gamely staved off the last bids of Joe Morris, Fighting Bob, and Boola Boola. It was a four-horse race down to the wire with 40,000 screaming fans—urging on their favorite.

Meridian, as a six-year-old, poses in a field at the end of his career. His tail is short, in the style of the era.

Meridian, the son of Broomstick, who held the world record for one-and-a-half-miles and also sired Halma, the 1895 Derby winner, won the Derby under questionable circumstances. Meridian led from "wire to wire" in the 1911 Derby, but the favorite, Governor Gray, the only other serious contender, was held back too far and for too long in the first half of the race. When he was allowed his head, he came on gamely, but Meridian had enough in reserve to hold off the challenge.

After the race, Capt. James T. Williams, one of the co-owners of Governor Gray, accused jockey Roscoe Troxler of deliberately giving his horse an inadequate ride. The imbroglio became even messier when it was reported that a Chicago bookmaker, Charley Ellis, had given Troxler a sum of money after the race. The sixty-five-year-old Williams apparently "attacked" Ellis near the Churchill Downs paddock and knocked off his hat with his cane. During the subsequent investigation, Ellis claimed he only loaned Troxler a few dollars. Nevertheless, Col. Matt Winn, Downs chairman, fined Ellis $100 for improper behavior.

Jesse Conley on Colston placed third and was the last black to ride in the Derby, which had been so dominated by black jockeys and trainers in its early years, notably Isaac Murphy, Willie Simms, and Jimmy Winkfield.

Meridian was a fine horse with a long record of stakes wins, including the National Handicap and Frontier Stakes as a three-year-old, and four more stakes at four and five. He was second in the Queens County Handicap and third in the Brookdale Handicap and the Yonkers Handicap at the age of six.

Carroll Shilling hustles the tiring Worth, who led all the way and held off the last efforts of
Duval and Flamma, the only filly in the race.

After Friday night's heavy rainfall, turfman Maj. T. C. McDowell thought it best to scratch The Manager, who did not run well in the mud, which left the field wide open for Worth in the thirty-eighth running. The colt was bought as a yearling by C. T. Worthington for $425, and was then turned over to the Gallagher Brothers for breaking. They were so impressed with the colt that they purchased him.

Worth won his first two races, was runner-up in an allowance race, and then enjoyed a streak of 7 wins. By Kentucky's spring racing season, Worth attracted the attention of many horsemen, including Frank Taylor, trainer for H. C. Hallenbeck, the wealthy New Yorker who then paid $3,500 for him. Worth closed his two-year-old season by winning a $10,000 private sweepstakes. The brown colt by Knight of the Thistle was proclaimed the two-year-old champion of 1911 with earnings of $16,645. He won 10 of 11 starts.

After a slow start, Worth took the lead in the 1912 Derby and maintained an easy advantage under restraint, according to instructions from trainer F. M. Taylor to jockey, Shilling. Meanwhile, Duval, a Kentucky horse, was gradually wearing down the field. He came alongside Worth and the two battled it out—with Johnny Loftus on Flamma, the only filly, making his move at them too late. The pair out front continued to duel, though Shilling never used the whip he held at the ready. Duval's nose was at Worth's throatlatch when Worth stumbled. The crowd groaned, but Shilling held Worth together and they flashed under the wire, as East beat West one more time.

Carroll Shilling topped the list of leading jockeys in 1912 but Worth's career was abbreviated. He died as a three-year-old.

DONERAIL * May 10, 1913

Owner-trainer T. P. Hayes and jockey Roscoe Goose pose with pride in front of Donerail, the 91 to 1 long shot.

Donerail paid $184.90 for a $2.00 win ticket in 1913—the longest odds and biggest payoff ever. Owner Tom Hayes had decided to run the bay colt "just for the hell of it." It is one of the charms of racing that anything can happen, that anyone can win, as in 1973 when trainer Harrison Johnson stunned Saratoga by winning the rich Hopeful Stakes with Gusty O'Shay, once claimed at Charles Town racetrack for $5,000.

Past the stands the first time in the thirty-ninth Derby, the favorite, Ten Point, was in the lead with Foundation 2 lengths back. Few noticed that Donerail was in the race. It was a two-horse contest up to the half-mile, when the little Louisville boy, Roscoe Goose, who had been coasting in sixth on Donerail, realized he was shortening the distance to the front. His mount was running smoothly, and by the stretch he was up with the leaders. Challenging and meeting every challenge, Donerail got his head and neck in front, and by the wire a half of his body showed clear of the rest.

Donerail won for Hayes, making him the second and last man ever to breed, train, and own a Derby winner. Not only that, Donerail set a new track record for the one-and-a-quarter miles, covering the distance in 2:14 ⅘. The horse had done nothing better than third in two prior stakes. Roscoe Goose, however, had won 85 races that year and he set a record in death as in life. At the age of eighty-one he left an estate of $1.1 million—the wealthiest jockey of his era.

Goose began his great career inauspiciously, driving a delivery wagon, and ended it as a trainer who, among many successes to his credit, gave Charles Kurtsinger his first ride. Kurtsinger went on to win the roses twice—first with Twenty Grand in 1931 and then with War Admiral in 1937.

OLD ROSEBUD * May 9, 1914

Old Rosebud with Johnny McCabe up in a montage with John Madden, who bred not only Old Rosebud but the first Triple Crown winner, Sir Barton (1919 Derby). All were foaled in the same red and black trimmed barn at his Hamburg Place near Lexington.

Old Rosebud was the first of five Derby winners bred by John Madden: Sir Barton (1919), Paul Jones (1920), Zev (1923), and Flying Ebony (1925). Madden, however, had let Old Rosebud go as a yearling for $500. (He owned only one winner in the Derby—Plaudit, in 1898.) So successful was Old Rosebud's first season that H. C. "Ham" Applegate turned down an offer of $30,000 for the bay gelding. As a two-year-old, Old Rosebud started 14 times, was second in two races, and won the rest, making him the two-year-old champion of that season.

Since rain had not let up all night before Derby Day 1914, at dawn the track superintendent, Tom Young, ordered his men to buy all the sponges available in Louisville and mop up the track by hand. With this feat accomplished, the track was so fast that Old Rosebud set a record of 2:03⅖ that would stand until 1931.

"Hurry back, Johnny," called a stable boy to McCabe as he left the Downs paddock on the favorite. Old Rosebud burst to the lead and cut to the inside rail with Hodge hot on his heels. At the top of the stretch, Old Rosebud led Hodge who led the others. Bronzewing, the only filly in the race, was running "like a wild horse," picking up horses at the rear, and was making for Hodge when the race ended. McCabe had opened Old Rosebud up to an 8-length lead at the wire and smashed Donerail's record of 1913 by 1⅖ seconds.

Old Rosebud, plagued by lameness, went on to race more seasons than any other thoroughbred on record except for Exterminator (1918 Derby). Unraced at four and five due to a bowed tendon, he resurfaced at six and won 26 of his last 63 starts. He ran a total of 80 races and won 40. Old Rosebud fell victim to the fate of most geldings then. Having no future earning power as stallions, they were raced as long as possible. Still running at the age of eleven, Old Rosebud snapped a foreleg going to the front and had to be destroyed.

REGRET * May 8, 1915

The lovely chestnut filly Regret, with Joe Notter on board in front of the twin spires of Churchill Downs.

On May 8, 1915, Harry Payne Whitney's Regret became the first filly ever to win the Kentucky Derby. Regret, a star from the beginning of her career, had won as a two-year-old the Saratoga Special, Sanford Memorial Handicap, and Hopeful Stakes at Saratoga, the only three races she had been entered in, and all against colts. The Kentucky Derby was the first race of the great filly's third season. Despite a family loss when his brother-in-law drowned on the *Lusitania* the day before the Derby, H. P. Whitney, who had started eighteen horses in Derbies (more than any other owner), started Regret.

Whitney feared that Regret might become skittish among the fifteen colts, the largest Derby field to date, and bolt on the first turn. But jockey Joe Notter, working on his season's winning percentage of .38, put her on the lead and in the clear immediately.

The daughter of Broomstick and granddaughter of Ben Brush, Regret took the lead at the start and never relinquished it. At the last eighth, she drew away from the nearest contender and won by 2 lengths easing up. Harry Payne Whitney said, "She has won the greatest race in America and I am satisfied."

Regret competed through her fifth year, when she won the Gazelle Handicap and came second in the Brooklyn Handicap. Nineteen years after she had won the Derby, Regret died without producing a foal worthy of its mother.

The years of Donerail, Old Rosebud, and Regret marked a significant turning point in the history of the Derby. Donerail had won at such astounding odds and set a track record. Old Rosebud had shattered that record the following year, and Regret had trounced fifteen males and become the first filly to win. No longer could the Eastern racing establishment ignore their Southern peers. Churchill Downs had become the center of the Southern track establishment and the Derby was in truth the greatest race in the country again.

Bryant 80 ©

*Johnny Loftus gives George Smith a morning "blowout" past a sixteenth pole at Churchill Downs
prior to his Derby win. Portraits of jockey Johnny Loftus and owner John Sanford (insert).*

One of the headlines the day after the forty-second Derby read "Whitney Out of Money," referring to Harry Payne's lack of luck with either Thunderer or Dominant, with whom he had wanted to repeat his win of the year before.

The Churchill Downs flower gardens were at their best, ablaze with red geraniums. Twelve three-year-olds had been entered for the 1916 contest and nine went to the post. Harry Payne Whitney's entry of Dominant and Thunderer were favored, and Thunderer was undefeated. George Smith, John Sanford's black colt, had drawn the number 8 post position.

George Smith was cleverly saved for the first three-quarters of a mile then went to the front, where he seemed to be safe until Star Hawk, making up incredible distances from way behind the pack, challenged him in the stretch. Supporters of both horses screamed themselves hoarse. Whipped and spurred unmercifully, Star Hawk chased the leader down the stretch and, like a hound about to make the kill, was alongside his shoulder when they passed under the wire. George Smith won like a frightened deer.

A montage of track president, Matt Winn, and Pancho Villa with winner Omar Khayyam and jockey Charles Borel, in the winner's circle where it was then located in front of the grandstand.

Omar Khayyam was one of three Derby winners not born in this country (along with Tomy Lee and Northern Dancer). Foaled in England, the chestnut colt was purchased at Newmarket by the partnership of Billings and Johnson and sent to this country as a yearling. No one suspected he would win the Kentucky Derby at odds of 12 to 1. As a two-year-old, he had only 1 win to his credit and had been unplaced in his only start as a three-year-old prior to the Derby. After his win on May 12, Omar Khayyam won 7 more straight and became the three-year-old champion and leading money winner for 1917 with earnings of $49,070.

Starting the Derby slowly, Omar Khayyam gradually gained on the leaders and, saving ground on the far turn, was in contention with Ticket, who he outstayed at the finish, besting fourteen other entries in another well-filled Derby. Midway closed a long distance to take third place. Omar Khayyam collected $16,600 in this single effort and continued to run through his fifth year. He retired to stud with a career total of $58,436.

Col. Matt J. Winn not only ran Churchill Downs but several other racetracks throughout the country during his career. His travels often brought him into contact with widely known figures, including the notorious Mexican chieftain, Pancho Villa. Villa had a fancy for racing and assembled his string in the best way he knew how—by force. Winn had warned Ben Jones that Villa's men would be shopping at his barn and Jones had a groom heavily bandage one hindleg of his best horse, Lemon Joe. When Villa's henchmen saw the apparently broken-down animal, they took a horse that bore a resemblance to Jones's favorite.

Exterminator (left) with Willy Knapp works out with stablemate, Sun Briar, who had been first choice to run in the Derby.

W. S. Kilmer's Sun Briar was the hottest contender for the 1918 Derby. Exterminator had been purchased ten days prior to the classic as a workhorse for Sun Briar, and when the favorite failed to train well, Exterminator went to the post in his stablemate's place and won in the mud at 30 to 1. As a two-year-old, Exterminator had started 4 times and won 2 unimportant races. The Derby was his first start at three years.

That second Saturday in May Exterminator won easily. He moved up fast after the three-quarter mark and, slipping through on the rail, took the lead from Escoba, who finished second. War Cloud, the favorite, met with interference on both turns and came in fourth behind Viva America. Thirty thousand people, most of them in shock and disbelief and some of whom didn't know Exterminator was in the race, nonetheless cheered the courageous performance as the darkest of dark horses gave the best three-year-olds in the country a smart licking. It is not known if J. Cal Milam, the man who had sold Exterminator ten days before, was cheering.

In his long and distinguished career, the public grew to adore Exterminator and gave him names like "Old Bones," "Old Slim," and "Old Hatrack." Exterminator won at all distances, often under crushing weights, and was at his zenith at seven when he won 10 of 17 starts carrying 132 pounds in all but two races. The public continued to make him the favorite long after his prime had passed. Having started in 100 races and won 50, he was a folk hero who retired when he was nine with an earnings record of $252,996.

H. G.—for "Hard Guy"—Bedwell, trainer, holds Sir Barton in the winner's circle with grim determination. Johnny Loftus scowls from the saddle.

It was another plum in the pocket of Kentucky's greatest all-round horseman, breeder and trainer, John Madden, affectionately called "The Wizard." Bred by Madden in partnership with Vivian Gooch of England, J. K. L. Ross's Sir Barton triumphed in this forty-fifth running with ease and followed this victory by winning the Preakness and the Belmont Stakes, that trio of long-distance classics that columnist Charlie Hatton would later dub the "Triple Crown."

As the race began, Sir Barton broke well and took command, with Eternal, considered his only threat, running second, with Billy Kelly third. Sir Barton led until the final eighth where Loftus "shook him up" with his whip. Eternal faded into obscurity and Sir Barton triumphed 5 lengths to the good of Billy Kelly. When the chestnut colt crossed the Derby finish he was carrying 2½ pounds of overweight, some of which was assumed to be cocaine as Sir Barton was celebrated as one of the "great hopheads" of racing history. It was common in those days to "help a horse along." Ethics forbade only that a trainer run a horse "hot" one day and "cool" the next, thereby duping the bettors and sweetening their own purses. Many an old-timer reflects upon the pleasure of seeing his favorite parade in the paddock "with all his lights turned on."

Johnny Loftus piloted Sir Barton for his Triple Crown wins in 1919, and the great team were best horse and rider of the year and leading money winners. At Kenilworth Park in 1920 they lost a match race to Man o' War by 7 lengths. It was "Big Red's" last race and a fitting way for him to retire, vindicating his only career loss of the year before when Loftus had ridden him to a defeat by Upset and was held responsible.

An attendant steadies Paul Jones in the winner's circle of the 46th Kentucky Derby with jockey Ted Rice.

Due to a press breakdown, the programs didn't arrive until just before the first race and the poor lad delivering them was mobbed, his jacket ripped, and his hat trampled by the zealous record crowd.

The 1920 Derby is best remembered as the Derby that Man o' War did not run in. His owner, Sam Riddle, thought the mandatory weight of 126 pounds—imposed this year for the first time—too heavy and too soon in a three-year-old's career, especially over a long distance. He wisely spared "Big Red," called by his faithful groom, Will Harburt, the "mostest hoss," and eventually retired him in 1920 as America's greatest racehorse. So popular was he in Lexington, that schoolchildren were directed to strew flowers in

his path as he ambled into retirement, an order remanded by Riddle, saying he was, after all, "just a horse."

Clyde van Dusen proved his sire probably could have handled the distance when he won the Derby in 1929. And another son, War Admiral, took the Triple Crown in 1937 under the 126-pound weight.

Paul Jones, the long-shot winner, was almost beaten by the only horse ever to outrun Man o' War—Upset—who looked the winner at the sixteenth pole but tired at the wire. Paul Jones was the sixth of seven geldings to win the Derby, the first gelding to win at level weights against colts, and ended his career after his fifth season with 14 wins in 65 starts.

Jockey Charles Thompson stands with Behave Yourself in his stall while H. J. "Derby Dick" Thompson and Col. E. R. Bradley, the owner-trainer team responsible for three more Derby wins, plot further strategy.

It was the opening of the Spring Meeting at the Downs and the unofficial opening of straw-hat season, with the Fifth Avenue Dobbs straw the most "correct." The four hotels in town were full past capacity. People slept in the halls and stood in lines to dine at restaurants. The inconveniences were a small price to pay for Derbytime in the spring. Col. Edward R. Bradley, a stone-faced gambler with a penchant for picking names for his horses beginning with the letter *B*, walked away from the 1921 Derby with close to $50,000 in prize money from his entries of Behave Yourself and Black Servant, who finished one and two. Harry Payne Whitney, whose entry of Prudery and Tryster had finished three and four, lost the $20,000 he so confidently dropped on their noses at the betting window.

Bradley had put the more successful jockey, Lyke, on Black Servant, and the less-known Thompson, on Behave Yourself. Thompson had done well on the less prestigious "Far West" circuit, notably in Juarez, and Bradley had just purchased his contract, never expecting him to outdo himself so completely on May 7. Behave Yourself's career was also undistinguished before and after the Derby, but for that short period both horse and rider were at their prime. Behave Yourself was the first to go out to the post and the first to come home.

Col. Bradley was reported to have been disappointed with the outcome of the Derby, as he had bet heavily on Black Servant. Behave Yourself had come second to Black Servant in the Blue Grass, a prep for the Derby. Bradley did, however, set two records, being the first to have owned and bred the one-two finishers in a Derby.

Over an undulating field of straw hats towers little Albert Johnson, aboard Morvich, the 1922 winner.

Morvich, the black colt who had won 11 of his 11 starts as a two-year-old, was a favorite with the crowd of 75,000.

A cry went up from the multitude in the stands and spread to the infield where thousands churned like a whirlpool turning to follow their horse. Morvich tore into the lead and running through the deafening corridor passed the stands with a 1½-length lead on Bradley's Busy American, the second favorite. But Busy American bobbled on the Clubhouse turn and was pulled up. My Play, a full brother to Man o' War, made a valiant reach for Morvich in the backstretch but was unsuccessful. Bet Mosie, who had lost a lot of ground going wide at both turns, made a tremendous effort at the last, closing the distance to lose by only a head to Morvich. Startle, the only filly in the race, lasted gamely for a mile, then faded.

When someone in the stands shouted that Morvich was done in on the far turn, it caused a near hysteria and a soldier fell into the governor's box. Owner Benjamin Block teetered on a chair as his horse came in and was escorted by a jubilant throng to the winner's circle.

Morvich never won another race after the Derby, the effort under so much weight being too great for many Derby winners, but Col. E. R. Bradley must have liked Albert Johnson's performance. He put him on Bubbling Over for the Derby of 1926, which he won.

Max Hirsch, the great trainer who would later run Bold Venture (1936), Assault (1946), and Middleground (1950) first under the Derby wire, may have regretted selling this colt he had purchased for a mere $4,000.

Earl Sande on Zev goes immediately to the front in the 49th Kentucky Derby.

A week prior to the Derby Zev finished twelfth in the Preakness. Owner Harry F. Sinclair, whose involvement in the Teapot Dome Scandal would later be revealed, and trainer Sam Hildreth didn't bother to show up for the Derby. Only two people seemed loyal to Zev: his jockey, leading rider Earl Sande, and a boy from Paris, Kentucky, who had dreamed that Zev won the Derby and came with his life's savings, $200, and put it on the brown colt's nose. With his $3,800 winnings he announced he would buy the family a home and take a long trip—all the way to Cincinnati.

Twenty-one of America's best three-year-olds came up to the starting web that year, the largest field in the race's history, among them the mud-running sprinter Zev, thought so out of place in the race by the press. Sande, who had argued with owner and trainer to let the horse run, used Zev's quick speed to put him on top instantly and kept him there. Effortlessly and smoothly, Zev ate up the track and led by 2½ lengths. Still running easily, he breezed around the oval with the rest of the field strung out behind him. Martingale, driving hard in second place, tried vainly to catch him but could never get closer than the 1½ lengths he trailed by at the finish. Zev came in at odds of 19 to 1.

The handsome big black colt was sired by The Finn. His dam was Miss Kearney. Earl Sande would soon triumph with another son of The Finn in 1925—Flying Ebony. The $272,008 won by Zev in 1923, including the Derby, made him the year's leading money winner. In addition, it was the most ever won in one year by an American racehorse.

BLACK GOLD * May 17, 1924

Black Gold steps out onto the track with John Mooney for the 50th Anniversary Kentucky Derby.

In 1909 Useeit, a pony-sized mare, raced against Belle Thompson, a larger, more experienced mare, at a dusty fairgrounds in Oklahoma. Although Useeit lost, she impressed Al Hoots, an Indian-Irish small-time rancher from Tulsa, who traded eighty acres of cattle grazing land for her. From the time of her purchase until 1916, the plucky mare raced 122 times, running in the money in 82 of those starts.

Her career ended abruptly on February 22, 1919, when she was claimed in a race in Mexico. Hoots refused to honor the claim, as there had been a gentlemen's agreement among the other owners not to claim Useeit, his love for the mare being common knowledge. Hoots chased off the waiting groom with a shotgun, packed the mare on a freight train to Oklahoma, and was instantly barred from racing. As Hoots lay dying the following year, he made his Osage Indian wife, Rosa, promise she would keep Useeit, breed her to Black Toney, Ed Bradley's great stallion, and run the result in the Kentucky Derby. Useeit was bred at Bradley's Idle Hour farm in Lexington and a dark foal was born on February 17, 1921, and named Black Gold for the oil that oozed in abundance out of Oklahoma soil.

In spite of mismanagement and bad training on the part of Hedley Webb, who often ran Black Gold when he was dead lame, the colt won half his starts as a two-year-old and went off the favorite in the fiftieth "Run for the Roses," the phrase invented that year by Bill Corum, who would take over track management in 1949. Black Gold came down the stretch with Chilhowee, Beau Butler, and Altawood, all four within a head's distance of each other. Black Gold pulled away by a half-length at the wire and made Rosa Hoots the second woman in history to run a Derby winner.

Sporadically lame, Black Gold was raced through his fourth season and retired to stud, where he proved to be sterile, and was returned to racing. In January 1928, the valiant Kentucky Derby winner broke a leg at the New Orleans Fair Grounds and was destroyed. A career that started at one fairground and ascended to the supreme pinnacle of American racing ended at another where he lies today.

A portrait of the powerful 51st Derby winner. The massive chest, sloping shoulder, and dropped rump, much like Secretariat's, made for his success. (Inset) The young Earl Sande.

In 1925, the Derby was a media event. Serious young men had wheeled in all kinds of technical equipment and had strung miles of wiring up to the top of the stands. "Credo" Harris, the director of WHAS Radio in Louisville, would announce the first broadcast of the Kentucky Derby. Over 6 million listeners worldwide were expected to tune in. The Derby was rapidly becoming a national sporting and social event, a triumph of the business and promotional talents of President Matt Winn who said, "My first love is the Kentucky Derby, and I've seen to it that the owners of three-year-olds with box office appeal flirt with no other stake but the Derby when Derbytime comes around."

Bill Corum's phrase, "Run for the Roses," had been picked up by newspapers and stations everywhere. This year's Derby resembled that of 1923. Although Earl Sande had persuaded Harry Sinclair to run Zev and won with

him then, he could not get a ride for 1925. Turfwriters intervened, asking Gifford A. Cochran to start his Flying Ebony that Sande might ride. He acquiesced as a token of good will. Like Zev, Flying Ebony had been sired by The Finn at Madden's Hamburg Place.

As the horses paraded to the post, the heavens opened up and turned the track into a sea of mud—just the stuff Flying Ebony liked best. The rain stopped as fast as it had started, but not before ruining the chances of the favorite, Quatrain, who despised the slop and finished up the track. Sande took Flying Ebony to the front just as he had done with his brother in '23, leading all the way around against the field of over twenty horses. Captain Hal pushed his nose in front twice but gave in to Flying Ebony in the stretch. It was the first time a horse from the pari-mutuel field had won. Had he not been included, his odds would have been impressive.

Bubbling Over, second from the right with the shadow-roll noseband he always wore, goes to the front at the start of the 52nd Kentucky Derby.

Kentuckian E. R. Bradley had a thing about the letter *B,* starting with a horse he named Bad News who traveled very fast. His busy B's had a red letter year in 1926 with Bagenbaggage, Boot to Boot and Bubbling Over.

Bubbling Over was 7 for 10 and always in the money during his freshman campaign. However, the freshman championship laurels had gone to Pompey—considered to be Bubbling Over's main rival. Yet in the fifty-second running, Bubbling Over had no real competition. Albert Johnson got him out in front immediately, set a torrid pace, and galloped home the winner by 5 lengths. Bubbling Over's stablemate, Bagenbaggage, got a slow start but was running quickly at the end for the place money. It was the second time Col. Bradley had sent out both the winner and the runner-up, having done so in 1921 with Behave Yourself and Black Servant. It was also a double for jockey Albert Johnson, who won with Morvich in 1922.

New York Mayor Jimmy Walker was there to present the trophy to the winner. Later he said, "I thought being elected mayor was the greatest thrill, but shucks, this is *the* thrill."

Bubbling Over broke down after the Derby and never raced again. But he was to make his presence felt in the Derby again when his son Burgoo King won in 1932.

"Ed" Bradley and his trainer, "Derby Dick" Thompson, dominated the Derby from his first entry in 1920 until his last in 1945. He often had as many as three horses in the classic, and if you didn't know what to bet, you "Bet Bradley." Bubbling Over, Burgoo King, and Brokers Tip (1933) all came home first for Bradley's Idle Hour farm.

Bradley was a gentleman gambler who backed down for no man, armed or not. In 1898 he opened his fabulous Palm Beach Club. Its popularity was attributed to the personality of its owner who never drank, swore, or smoked.

Harry Payne Whitney and James R. Keene, each of whom topped the country's list of leading owners many times, in front of Linus McAtee on Whiskery in Whitney's pale blue and coffee-brown silks.

Under a sky that alternately cleared and rained, the colorfully crowded stands seemed to glow and dim like houselights. The barrier flew up and the race was off to a fast start. "Chick" Lang on Jock literally flew to the lead and by the half-mile was 5 lengths in front. Meanwhile, Whiskery was deep in the pack but moved up to third position at the three-quarter pole. Osmand was running second as the three leaders hit the top of the stretch. Jock tired, leaving Whiskery and Osmand with Earl Sande driving hard to duel to the wire, where Whiskery prevailed by a blinkered head under a strong ride from "Pony" McAtee.

This was the second Derby win for Harry Payne Whitney, his talented filly Regret having triumphed in the 1915 running. The Whitney family would enter the Derby a total of fifty-nine times and win twice more with Mrs. Payne Whitney's Twenty Grand (under her watermelon and pink-striped silks) in 1931 and Shut Out in 1942.

Had a quick-thinking groom not blocked Whiskery's hind foot from wedging between his stall door and its frame as the horse rolled the morning of the race, there wouldn't have been a Whitney winner and one that is so closely tied into Derby history. The 1896 winner, Ben Brush, was grandsire to both Meridian (1911), and Regret (1915), who were by Broomstick. Broomstick sired Whiskbroom II, who sired Whiskery. Prudery, Whiskery's dam, had run third in the Derby of 1921, and her sire, Peter Pan was the grandsire of Black Gold (1924). Whiskery was retired to stand at stud, where he did not prove himself. He was returned to racing, from which he was retired again, and was used as a field hunter until his natural death.

Reigh Count with "Chick" Lang up is led from the paddock where a field of straw hats envelopes the old Secretary's stand. (Insert) Owner, Mrs. John D. Hertz, the third woman after Mrs. C. E. Durnell and Rosa Hoots to own a Derby winner.

Reigh Count didn't win a race until his seventh start. When the colt finally did break his maiden, owner Willis Sharpe Kilmer was willing to let him go for "a pittance" to John D. Hertz, the Austrian immigrant who parlayed a few used cars into the Yellow Cab Company and later Hertz Rent-a-Car. Hertz had seen Reigh Count bite or "savage" another horse at the wire. It made a lasting impression on the former pugilist. The decision was made to run the horse under Mrs. Hertz's name.

Trainer Barney Michell quickly brought the "sulky" colt to hand for several important wins as a two-year-old. He then took an unusual route to the Derby, bringing Reigh Count up to the race on workouts alone. There, twenty-one rivals came to face the colt in the largest Derby to date. The crowd made Reigh Count the clear favorite. Jockey "Chick" Lang rated him patiently behind the leaders, picked up horses through the backstretch, and got a head in front at the top of the stretch. At the wire Reigh Count was 3 lengths the best of Misstep with speed in reserve.

Reigh Count went on to win many important stakes as a three-year-old. However, he did become a victim of "the graveyard of favorites" when he came up last in the Travers at Saratoga that August. He campaigned in England at four, winning the Coronation Cup and gaining a place in the Ascot Gold Cup. He was a most successful sire for the Hertzes, but his offspring included no Derby winners until Hertz bucked conventional wisdom and bred Reigh Count to an overraced, undistinguished mare named Quickly. The resulting ugly duckling of a foal was named Count Fleet, eventual winner of the Triple Crown (1943), who sired Count Turf, winner of the 1951 Derby.

CLYDE VAN DUSEN * May 18, 1929

Clyde Van Dusen holds off Naishapur in the stretch run of the 55th Kentucky Derby.

The radio broadcasts that had begun just four years before had branched into a worldwide network bringing the Derby into homes everywhere. Despite the Wall Street crash, Derby enthusiasts will remember 1929 as the year that Jockey Linus "Pony" McAtee came back to Churchill Downs to repeat his victory of two years before on Whiskery. Only this time he rode a much smaller horse, an unusually high-spirited gelding named after his trainer, Clyde Van Dusen.

The day that jockey McAtee arrived to meet his Derby mount, trainer Clyde Van Dusen met him at the jockey's quarters to prepare him for his first glimpse of the horse. Trainer Van Dusen tactfully explained to the jockey that although Van Dusen was very small, he was fast and if McAtee could give him a good ride, he could win. In spite of the preparation, McAtee's mouth dropped when he saw the size of the gelded son of Man o' War.

The low odds that day were on Col. E. R. Bradley's entry of Blue Larkspur and Bay Beauty, who headed a field of twenty-one outstanding thoroughbreds. Just at post time the heavens opened up, making the track a river of mud. With a rainfall of 1.17 inches that day the fifty-fifth Derby became one of the wettest on record. Clyde Van Dusen (the horse) had drawn post position number 20 and at the bell took off like a rocket. He was leading by the first quarter and saved ground while setting the pace. Naishapur, slow to start and racing wide, began moving up after going five-eighths, was blocked in the stretch, but came up again from twelfth place past Panchio, who was running second. At the finish it was Clyde Van Dusen by 2 lengths, Naishapur second by 3 and Panchio third. Blue Larkspur, the favorite, who had been shod for a dry track, finished fourth. Clyde Van Dusen had won for his owner $53,950. After Clyde Van Dusen's successful four-year racing career, he was retired as a pensioner, a kindness now extended to geldings.

GALLANT FOX * May 17, 1930

A montage of trainer James "Sunny Jim" Fitzsimmons with Earl Sande on Gallant Fox and owner William Woodward of Belair Stud resting against President Roosevelt's limousine at Saratoga.

The great "Earl of Sande" had suffered severe leg injuries in a fall at Saratoga following his second Derby win on Flying Ebony in 1925 and had retired to train. William Woodward, determined to have Sande on his Gallant Fox, coaxed him out of retirement and they won the Preakness Stakes coming up to the Kentucky Derby.

Gallant Fox, an impressive bay colt by Sir Gallahad III, was the crowd favorite of the fifteen three-year-olds from the best stables in the country. Both Fitzsimmons and Sande had expressed their confidence in the colt. According to the odds makers, the only horse Gallant Fox had to beat was E. F. Prichard's Tannery.

A persistent drizzle did not alter the condition of the track. The horses were led into the stalls of the first mechanical gate used at the Downs and, when the bell clanged, got off to a perfect start. Gallant Fox was in tight quarters for the first three-eighths of a mile then broke loose from the pack and swung wide to the outside. Passing horse after horse, he took over the lead in the backstretch. From then on the race belonged to him. At the finish, he led by 2 lengths to the good of Gallant Knight, who had made a strong bid at the mile but couldn't keep pace with "that handy guy named Sande: bootin' a winner in." Tannery, a victim of the blistering pace, finished "up the track."

Gallant Fox won the Belmont Stakes to become the second Triple Crown winner, after Sir Barton in 1919, and would initiate a ten-year dominance of the Derby by Woodward, Fitzsimmons, and Belair. The "Fox of Belair" would be the only Triple Crown winner to sire a Triple Crown winner, Omaha, whose triple came in 1935. Another offspring, Johnstown, would come close with a 10-length win in the 1939 Derby and triumph in the Belmont Stakes. In this third Derby win, Sande tied Isaac Murphy's win record, but outdistanced him by going on to take the Triple Crown. Sande's record would stand until 1938 when the master of the craft, Eddie Arcaro, would start his Derby blitz of five wins with Lawrin in 1938.

*Twenty Grand at the head of the pack on the far turn in Mrs. Whitney's pink and black silks
barely misses hitting spectators who pile on top of each other on the infield rail.*

Tens of thousands of Derby fans had arrived for the fifty-seventh running and Bowman Field was packed with private two-seaters and the "giant" thirty-passenger Fokker transports. By noon the grandstand was filled beyond capacity with dapper gentlemen and lovely women in silk shantung, chiffons, and polka dots that blended in a shifting cataract of color.

The track was lightning fast. Not only did Twenty Grand whip through the mile-and-a-quarter distance in a record time of 2:01⅘, but Gallant Knight, second in the Derby the year before, had thrilled the crowd in the race just before this Derby by setting a world record for 6½ furlongs in 1:16⅖.

An even dozen of the nation's best three-year-olds paraded to the mechanical gate without the wonderful Equipoise (scratched due to an injury), who had pushed Twenty Grand to a record for the mile the year before in a nose-to-nose duel. Twenty Grand started slowly. Taking him to the outside, Kurtsinger gradually brought him past the pack after the ½-mile and wore down Sweep All at the front. With a tremendous show of energy he widened the gap to 4 lengths and passed under the wire with speed to spare.

It was the first of two Derby wins for Kurtsinger, who would triumph again on War Admiral in 1937. Twenty Grand won the Wood Memorial, Belmont Stakes, Travers, and Jockey Club Gold Cup that year, then was retired to stud, where he did not distinguish himself. He was returned to racing in his seventh year but without much success.

Eugene James goes to the post on Burgoo King, in E. R. Bradley's green and white silks, past the crowded extension of the grandstand. (Insert) Colonel Bradley and "Derby Dick" Thompson.

The Depression was showing some effect on the Derby by 1932, at least in the wagering, which this year would be less than half of three years before. The favorite for the fifty-eighth Run for the Roses was Loma Stable's great colt, Tick On, over the Bradley entry of Burgoo King and Brother Joe. Burgoo King, an impressive colt by Bubbling Over, Bradley's 1926 winner, was named for James T. Looney, who popularized the local stew across the nation and was dubbed the "Burgoo King." Although Burgoo King had not won a stakes race in his two-year-old career, Bradley was willing to bet anyone $5,000 that he could beat their horse the first time they met as three-year-olds. There were no takers.

Just prior to the start, 5,000 fans broke through the back side fence and poured into the infield as the police stood by helpless. For 15½ minutes the field of twenty churned at the start with Tick On creating most of the disturbance. Finally off, Economic took the lead and dominated the race until the top of the stretch. Burgoo King, possibly feeling the effects of his cod liver oil and fish liver diet, fairly leaped from the pack and with a tremendous stretch drive passed Economic and pulled away to a 5-length win.

The nineteen-year-old Eugene James from Louisville spoke proudly of his win into the Movietone microphone, with the same direct forthrightness that carried Burgoo King down the stretch for Bradley's second Derby triumph win. Burgoo King would go on to win the Preakness and retire to produce many stakes winners until his death in 1946 at the age of seventeen.

Herb Fisher on Head Play (left) grabs for Brokers Tip's saddlecloth as he drives past him on the inside rail. Jockey Don Meade tries to push Fisher away in the homestretch of the "Rodeo Derby."

E. R. Bradley, the first man to breed and own three Derby winners, never expected to do it a fourth time with Brokers Tip, who never won another race. Brokers Tip, the son of Black Toney, sire of Black Gold (1924) was born with a half-deformed foot and couldn't stand on his own as a weanling. Shod with the weak foot raised on leather pads, Brokers Tip made it to the races at two but never won.

Head Play, bought by Willie Crump for $500, was sold to Mrs. Silas B. Mason the day before the Derby for $30,000 plus 15 percent of the purse if he won (and he was favored).

A light breeze groomed the track to perfection as the bugle called the thirteen horses from the paddock. The field got off to a good start. Head Play went to the front while Brokers Tip stayed at the rear. At the top of

the stretch, Jockey Fisher, unaware of Brokers Tip coming up behind him, took Head Play wide to ride out Charley O, a fatal mistake as Don Meade took the opportunity to bring Brokers Tip in on the rail. Fisher, thinking he had the race won, came back in to battle neck and neck with Brokers Tip but was "out of gas" from running wide, and made his desperate lunge to stop Meade. Past the wire, Fisher stood in his stirrups and slashed at Meade with his whip. As the official sign went up declaring Brokers Tip the winner, Fisher sat down and cried. Back in the jockey's room, he attacked Meade and fought viciously until reporters and valets broke them up. Though "foul riding" was not uncommon, it was usually done with more discretion. Derby mania had simply carried Fisher away.

Cavalcade in front of one of the barns at Brookmeade trimmed in the blue and white colors of the "Mistress of Brookmeade," Mrs. Isabel Dodge Sloan (insert).

In 1934, Isabel Dodge Sloan, of the automobile industry fortune, was named leading owner—a first in racing history for a woman. Inheriting $7 million on the death of her father, John F. Dodge, Mrs. Sloan went a'-racing, first with steeplechasers and then on the flat. She purchased Cavalcade (who was conceived in England but born in this country) at Saratoga as a yearling for $1,200.

The Derby enjoyed a capacity crowd, swelling to overcapacity when gate-crashers rushed past the token police force. The next year the National Guard would be called in to maintain order and put an end to gate-crashing for all time. The media was out in force with both WHAS for CBS and WAVE for NBC covering the event along with a sea of popping flashbulbs and clicking shutters.

Thirteen horses burst from the gate and Mata Hari jumped to a lead she held at the mile. Cavalcade, who had broken slowly, was steadily creeping toward the front with Discovery hot on his heels. At the top of the stretch Discovery had captured the lead, with Cavalcade alongside. Cavalcade wore down Discovery and pulled away to a handsome victory. The usually dignified and sedate Mrs. Sloan screamed herself silly.

Jockey Willie Garner had tried thirteen times to win the Derby, and had come the closest with a second on Misstep in 1928. After twenty years of riding races, his horse led in the Derby homestretch. It was also a satisfying victory for trainer R. A. Smith, who had inadvertently muffed his first try at the racing game. As a lad in 1887, he'd paid $210 at Sheepshead Bay for a runt of a colt, so badly did he want a horse of his own. Ridiculed for the young horse's appearance, Smith sold the colt, who later became Tenny, Salvator's great match-race rival.

OMAHA * May 4, 1935

Omaha with Willie "Smokey" Saunders strides out onto the track at Churchill Downs under the red and white polka-dot silks of William Woodward's Belair Stud.

The sixty-first running of the Kentucky Derby would be photographed by the Standard Gravure Corporation for reproduction in the *Courier-Journal* newspaper. The time needed to reproduce the event for the public would be only 1¾ hours, not exactly instant replay but a remarkable achievement for the times. The Derby betting pool climbed back to its $1 million mark of four years before and the gate-crashers were trounced by the National Guard.

In spite of the rain and the unseasonably cold weather, the stands were packed. The favorite that day carried the new but soon-to-be-famous silks of Calumet Farm, and the horse was Nellie Flag, the first filly favorite in the Derby, ridden by a jockey destined for immortality, Eddie Arcaro. Omaha, the chestnut son of Triple Crown winner Gallant Fox, was also favored along with E. R. Bradley's Boxthorn. Eighteen horses started from the so-called me-chanical gate, in this case an arrangement of free-standing padded dividers with a wire strung from end to end in front that sprung upward at the bell. The Kentucky-born Omaha avoided the crowding that caught Nellie Flag and, running wide, took command at the half-mile and romped on home, much in the style of his dad five years before. "Smokie" Saunders said it was "a cinch" and passed out his roses. "He won in a romp," gushed his owner, the staid president of the New York Jockey Club, William Woodward. Then he hugged a reporter.

Gallant Fox never had the chance to show his full potential, but through his son, Omaha, ran and triumphed again over the same courses. With wins in the Preakness and the Belmont Stakes, Omaha made his sire the only Triple Crown winner to sire a Triple Crown winner. Like so many great racehorses, however, Omaha was a failure at stud.

Brevity goes to his knees as Bold Venture starts well in the brown and white colors of M. L. Schwartz at the beginning of the Kentucky Derby.

The sixty-second Run for the Roses was strewn with thorns. The favorite, Brevity, fell at the start. Eventual Horse of the Year, Granville, unseated his rider. World record holder for the mile and an eighth, Indian Broom, was badly blocked. Bold Venture was in close quarters too, but jockey Ira "Babe" Hanford steered him out of trouble and into the lead. He Did lost all hope of a late rally when a long-armed spectator standing on the inner rail of the last turn reached out and grabbed jockey Charles Kurtsinger's whip. At the wire, it was Bold Venture holding a head advantage over the colt that many thought had run the best race—Brevity, who overcame his stumble at the start, was forced to race wide, yet covered a tremendous amount of ground to miss catching the winner by a head. After the race three jockeys were barred from the track for fifteen days for rough riding, including Ira Hanford.

Though trained by the esteemed Max Hirsch, Bold Venture appeared outclassed by the talented Derby field. He had never won a stakes, and was being ridden by an apprentice jockey—no apprentice had ever won a Derby. Bold Venture was to prove, though, that his performance in the Derby was no fluke. A week later he took the Preakness, withstanding another furious stretch duel, this time with Granville, who had managed to keep his jockey in the saddle. Bold Venture bowed a tendon after the Preakness and was retired. But the horse was lucky enough to be alive. On a trip back from Saragota, his railroad car had caught on fire. His groom, Rufus "Do Right" Scott, beat back the flames for mile after mile to save the colt's life.

War Admiral with Charles Kurtsinger up walks toward owner Sam Riddle and trainer George Conway.

By 1937, the Derby had become so popular and overcrowded that spectators made cheap cardboard periscopes in an attempt to get some view of the proceedings. Most heard, rather than saw, War Admiral's classic performance.

War Admiral's sire, Man o' War, may have been the greatest racehorse ever. But War Admiral was to do something he never did—win the Kentucky Derby. Sam Riddle, who owned and bred both, never cared for the Derby and had held Man o' War out of it. To him, Churchill Downs was an upstart track, and its long-distance classic came too early in the year for not quite mature three-year-olds.

On the small side like his mother, and something of a late bloomer like his father, War Admiral finally got going as a two-year-old, winning 3 out of 6, and was never out of the money. He was the favorite in this Derby over nineteen rivals—including the two-year-old champion, Pompoon—but War Admiral had a distinct aversion to the starting gate and held up the Derby start for 8½ minutes while his handlers tried to wedge him into his stall. But when the gates finally sprang open he was all business. He flew to the lead and stayed there to the wire, holding off Pompoon by almost 3 lengths.

"The Admiral's" Preakness win may have been the most exciting race of the year. He and Pompoon battled up to the stretch, neck and neck every step of the way except the last, where War Admiral got a nose in front. He then gave jockey Charles Kurtsinger, "the Flying Dutchman," a rocking-chair ride in his easy Belmont win—to become the fourth Triple Crown champion.

LAWRIN   *   May 7, 1938

A portrait of the 1938 Derby winner.

The big winner on Derby Day was Herbert M. Woolf. Not only did he own Lawrin, but he backed him heavily at attractive odds, cashing in an estimated $150,000 in pari-mutuel tickets. Herbert Woolf had been a prominent breeder of saddle breds, but witnessing the Derby of 1929 convinced him to acquire a stable of running horses. He campaigned the Kansas-bred Lawrin heavily, starting him 23 times before the Churchill Downs meet without impressive results. His jockey, Eddie Arcaro, was born in Cincinnati, weighing only three pounds. Sickly as a child, he toughened up at local "bush league" tracks in Kentucky.

As the race got underway, Arcaro rated his mount through the early going, hugging the rail and saving every bit of precious ground. By the top of the stretch Lawrin had the lead by 3 lengths, but with an eighth of a mile to go, his drive for the wire wilted and he started to drift out into the center of the track. Dauber was gaining with every stride, but the race was over before Dauber pulled even with the winner. The Derby win would remain the highlight of this Kansas shipper's career.

Mrs. Payne Whitney's contract with Arcaro allowed him to ride for other stables if Greentree was not entered, which is how Arcaro was free to ride Lawrin for trainer Ben Jones; Arcaro and Jones would collaborate on three more Derby wins.

© BRYANT '83

Johnstown as a stud in later years with his trainer, James "Sunny Jim" Fitzsimmons, as an older man.

New backstretch bleachers were opened in 1939 and 20,000 took advantage of the 50¢ admission and the $1 bets available there. A few dozen enterprising and fearless fans shinnied up telephone poles across the street from the track and lashed a crossbar between them. From that vantage point they watched Johnstown show why he was the overwhelming favorite.

Johnstown, nicknamed the "Old Man of the Mountains," counted four stakes among his 7 wins as a two-year-old. At three he set the track record at Jamaica Park for a mile and seventy yards, and equaled the course standard in the Wood. His odds were the shortest in thirty-four years, and the field of eight was the smallest of the last twenty-one Derbies.

Jockey James Stout got Johnstown out to the lead soon after the start, and there he stayed uncontested. The big Kentucky bred put on a show in the stretch, drawing clear to an 8-length advantage. Nick Wall, who rode El Chico, said, "All I'm thankful for is that Stout didn't whack Johnstown across the rear end once during the whole race, because, if he had'a, Johnstown would have won that race by a half-mile."

For Stout this impressive win was vindication for the 1936 Derby, in which he was unseated by Granville at the post. Johnstown was the third Kentucky Derby winner for trainer, "Sunny Jim" Fitzsimmons. And Johnstown's owner, William Woodward, in just ten years and with only six tries, had run three Derby winners (Gallant Fox, 1930, and Omaha, 1935). Great though he thought Johnstown was, Woodward was not ready to concede that this colt was the equal of his favorite, Gallant Fox.

Gallahadion, in the orange, chocolate, and white colors of Mrs. Ethel Mars of the Mars candy company, fights to outlast Bimelech in the stretch of the 66th Derby.

In 1940, a Bradley horse named Bimelech went off at even shorter odds than Johnstown had the year before. Bimelech was the shortest priced Derby horse since the advent of pari-mutuel wagering.

As "Derby Dick" Thompson, Bradley's first-string trainer, had died when Bimelech was two, the aging Bill Hurley took over his career. And where the first could be criticized for training too hard, Hurley had a tendency to train too soft. Left in Kentucky to fatten over the winter, Hurley put Bimelech into hard work to ready for the Blue Grass. The two-year-old champ won it easily but was strained after the race. Yet Hurley ran Bimelech two days later in the Derby trial, which he won, trouncing Gallahadion and other hopefuls. But the effort had ruined his Derby chances.

Gallahadion wore down his highly touted rival in the final furlong. The long-shot players in the crowd were rewarded with $74.20 for every $2.00

bet. Few had given this colt any chance to win, but trainer Roy Waldron had been predicting victory for his Gallahadion all week. Perhaps most surprised by the outcome was jockey Carroll Bierman. He had never been aboard Gallahadion, and considered Bimelech to be the best horse in America. His riding strategy was simple—to save all the ground he could. He negotiated Gallahadion to a 1½-length win.

It was a sweet victory for owner Ethel V. Mars, who had parlayed her husband's candy bar fortune into a top racing stable known as the "Stars of the Milky Way." Illness forced her to follow the proceedings over the radio. Her daughter said, "I'm sure mother would have fainted had she not already been in bed."

Gallahadion ran a few more respectable races, but would never again be a stakes winner.

WHIRLAWAY * May 3, 1941

Whirlaway, as a stallion at Calumet Farm where he was raised, strikes a handsome pose as owner Warren Wright proudly holds his lead shank. He was the first of eight Derby winners bred and run by Calumet and the first of their two Triple Crown champs.

The crowd of 100,000 for the sixty-seventh running poured almost $2 million into the pari-mutuel machines, the most wagered since 1926, and they were rewarded with a record-shattering performance. The paper the next day referred to Whirlaway's 8-length victory as a "blitzkrieg" and the battle for place "rear-guard action."

Whirlaway was bred for both the Epsom Derby, which his sire, Blenheim II had won, and this Derby which his great-grandsire, Ben Brush, had won. As a two-year-old, "Whirly" was impressive but had only won twice, by a neck each time, and never displayed the great stretch drive which would become his trademark. In the Blue Grass Stakes, a Derby prep race, he took the lead at the top of the stretch. Then his sire's crazy streak surfaced and he bore out so badly he wound up 6 lengths behind the winner. In the Derby Trial, he showed a startling burst of speed around the far turn but made a beeline for the outer rail instead of the finish. Trainer Ben A. Jones admitted that "Whirly" was "the dumbest horse I ever trained." When asked if Whirlaway was a half-wit, Jones replied, "I don't know, but he's making a half-wit out of me."

Jones did three things to correct Whirly's problem: he got Eddie Arcaro, a jockey known to have "good hands"; he and Arcaro trained him to run next to the inside rail (Jones on his white pony would plant himself just far enough out from the rail for a horse to slip through, then Arcaro would send Whirly down the stretch and through the gap) and he cut away part of the inside cup of the horse's blinkers, so he could see the rail. It all worked.

Whirlaway hung back in the early going but by the top of the Derby stretch he was clear by 3 lengths and made directly for the wire, putting a good 8 lengths between his long-flying tail and the rest. "Mr. Longtail" had taken ⅖ of a second off Twenty Grand's 1931 record for the one and one-fourth miles, and taking the Preakness and Belmont in stride he became the fifth to earn the Triple Crown in the twenty-two years of its existence. He won 5 more stakes that year and as a four-year-old took 11 more. But it wasn't just that he won, it was the way he won. "It was never any picnic to ride Whirlaway," said Arcaro. "Once he started to climb you just couldn't slow him down. It was like stepping on the accelerator of a big Cadillac. How he could pour it on!"

*Shut Out goes postward with Wayne Wright in the irons. Mrs. Payne Whitney (insert) became
the first woman to own two Derby winners, her first being Twenty Grand in 1931.*

The Derby crowd sported a new fashion look in 1942—uniforms. The soldiers, sailors, and marines, were reminders that most of the world was at war. In the betting shed both pari-mutuel tickets and war bonds were sold.

The crowd had picked the Greentree Stable entry as the favorite because of Devil Diver, and not because of his lightly regarded stablemate, Shut Out. Sharing the crowd's appraisal was jockey Eddie Arcaro. Even after piloting Shut Out to an impressive Blue Grass Stakes score, the Kentucky Italian chose Devil Diver for the Derby and gave Shut Out to a scrappy Idaho rider named Wayne Wright who wanted to make a comeback. Shut Out started off smartly, pressing the pace, and then drew clear in the stretch by over 2 lengths. Arcaro

and Devil Diver finished sixth. Arcaro chose Devil Diver again for the Preakness Stakes and again they finished behind Shut Out, who did not win this classic. He returned for the Belmont, this time with Arcaro, who had seen the light, and they won. The pair went on to repeat the performance in the Travers at Saratoga.

Shut Out was the last son of the great Equipoise. Like Man o' War, Equipoise won just about everything there was to win in horse racing but the Kentucky Derby, which he had been favored to win until he came up lame just prior to Derby Day. Like Man o' War and War Admiral, winning the Derby was a task Equipoise left to his son.

*Jockey Johnny Longden gives Count Fleet an early morning workout. Count Fleet made his owner,
Mrs. John Hertz, the second woman in Derby history to run two winners (Reigh Count, 1928),
after Mrs. H. P. Whitney's Twenty Grand in 1931 and her Shut Out the year before Count Fleet.*

The 1943 Derby crowd came to Churchill Downs in streetcars because of wartime gasoline restrictions. Not one of John Hertz's yellow cabs was in evidence when Count Fleet won the 1943 Derby.

Reigh Count had sired many winners but until "The Count," no champions. Before giving up on the stallion completely, Hertz bred Reigh Count, a "stayer," to speed in the form of a swift mare named Quickly. The resulting ugly duckling became something of a rogue. Hertz tried to unload Count Fleet several times, but jockey Johnny Longden realized that the colt was a "runner" and prevailed upon Hertz not to sell him, whereupon Hertz prevailed upon Longden to do the riding.

The Count started well at two, but then lost a couple of important stakes, including the Futurity, at Belmont, where he clung to a filly named Askmenow.

Said Longden, "For the last three-eighths he laid on Askemenow, and I couldn't drag him off." But that was to be the last defeat of his career.

He and nine rivals made it to Churchill Downs, where he got right out to the front, coasting to an easy 3-length win. In the Preakness, he stretched the winning margin to 8 lengths, and for the Belmont he drew clear by an incredible 25. He had warmed up for the third leg of the Triple Crown by romping in the Withers as well. But winning the Triple Crown was to be Count Fleet's last accomplishment as a racehorse. He had injured himself in the Belmont and was never able to return to the track. Like his sire, Reigh Count, Count Fleet also sired a Derby winner—1951 champion, Count Turf. It was the first three-generation sweep of the event.

PENSIVE * May 6, 1944

Pensive and Conn McCreary in the red and blue silks of Calumet Farm break from the gate.

The favorite May 6 was Greentree Stable's Stir Up with jockey Eddie Arcaro under contract to Greentree. Calumet's Pensive brought back memories of Cavalcade's 1934 Derby. Both were sired by and out of English horses. Cavalcade, by Lancegaye out of Hastily, had been imported to this country while still carried by Hastily. In 1940, England's Lord Astor sold a mare named Penicuik II to an American breeder, on the condition that Penicuik II be bred to Hyperion, the English Derby winner. Penicuik II was purchased by Warren Wright shortly before she foaled the chestnut colt, Pensive, who would become the Kentucky Derby's seventieth winner.

The condition of the track was good in spite of a 36-hour deluge, which had finally ended the afternoon before the race. Sixteen three-year-olds went to the post. Aboard Pensive, little Conn McCreary was looking for his first Derby win in 4 starts. The gates opened and Pensive was fourth in the early running. McCreary took Pensive back to thirteenth, but by the mile had moved him up to fifth on the inside. Hugging the rail, his chestnut coat gleaming, the big colt flew by the leaders as if they were standing still. At the finish, Pensive was ahead of his nearest rival by 4½ lengths. Stir Up and Arcaro finished third.

This was Calumet's second Derby win and the awesome winning machine that would take six more had begun to roll. It was trainer Ben A. Jones's third winner, putting him just one victory behind trainer "Derby Dick" Thompson of Idle Hour.

Fred Hooper holds Hoop Jr. with Eddie Arcaro up. Trainer I. H. Parke and friends pose in their flamboyant suits and hats.

Because of a war-time effort to curb unnecessary transportation, the Derby was run almost a month late. Over 80,000 filled Churchill Downs. Eddie Arcaro would win his third Derby, equaling the records of Isaac Murphy and Earl Sande. Murphy had won his third in 1891 and Sande, back from retirement, won his third on Gallant Fox in 1930.

Arcaro and Calumet's Ben Jones had scored two Derbies together, but in 1944 Jones pulled ahead when he assigned Conn McCreary to Pensive, who beat Arcaro on Stir Up. In this Derby, Arcaro evened the score with Hoop Jr. and beat the Ben Jones-trained Pot O'Luck. The team of Jones and Arcaro would win again in 1948 and 1952.

Pot O'Luck was the slight favorite over Hoop Jr., and the entire field was soaked to the skin. The track was lost in water. A healthy roar went up from the infield and the stands when the horses broke from the gate. Starting from the twelfth "hole," Hoop Jr. was in charge by the first quarter, with Buymeabond keeping pace just behind. Pot O'Luck had moved up quickly to eighth and was driving hard. Running almost without effort in the stretch, Hoop Jr. opened the gap to 6 lengths over Pot O'Luck at the wire.

Hoop Jr. was the first yearling purchased by Fred Hooper, the Florida contractor who said after the Derby win, "I never thought I'd make it so quick." Having won the Wood Memorial, the Kentucky Derby, and placed second in the Preakness, Hoop Jr. was retired to stud service.

In the paddock, jockey Warren Mehrtens, trainer Max Hirsch, and Robert Kleberg of the King Ranch admire Assault before Mehrtens gets a "leg up."

Over 105,000 war-weary Americans made their way to Churchill Downs to the first peacetime Kentucky Derby since Whirlaway's. A move to ban liquor from the race meeting was quashed. To women especially, the 1946 race will be remembered as the "Hat Derby." The Hedda Hopper variations caused women's heads to turn but annoyed serious horsemen whose views were blocked. One hat that could not go unnoticed was an extravaganza of apples, flowers, and ivy in triple tiers. Another featured turtles.

Robert Kleberg of the King Ranch, Texas, had bought the Max Hirsch-trained Bold Venture (Derby, 1936) from M. L. Schwartz for stud purposes and got Assault and Middleground from him. Both won the Derby under Hirsch's guidance. Assault became one of the top horses of the century, as he won the Preakness and Belmont, and thus became the seventh Triple Crown king, in spite of his deformed foot. [Brokers Tip had won the Derby (1933) with a bad foot but did nothing else.]

The race that day was never even close. The "Club-footed Comet," as he was affectionately called, started from a good post position, stayed with the leaders for the first mile and, turning for the stretch, effortlessly skimmed through on the rail. He was 2½ lengths in front at the one-sixteenth pole and, at the finish, he was 8 lengths to the good of Spy Song with Hampden third.

Jet Pilot enjoying his retirement.

It was still the Big Band era. While the "chic" partied at the famous Galt House, Sealbach, or Brown Hotel, others in "zoot suits" and fringes whooped it up to the beat of washboard bands. The parties continued for a week until the dawn of Derby Day.

The year before the seventy-third running, a disastrous fire had destroyed most of Main Chance Farm's stable of two-year-olds valued at $282,000. Luckily, Jet Pilot had just been shipped to Churchill Downs, with Mrs. Graham's Derby hopefuls for 1946. He won his first time out as a two-year-old at the Downs and 3 more times in 11 outings to return to Churchill for the 1947 Derby.

The heavy favorite to win was C. V. Whitney's Phalanx. Also favored was Calumet's Faultless, ridden by Eddie Arcaro, now back on the team with Ben Jones. Jet Pilot, sired by Blenheim II, Whirlaway's sire, took command of the race in much the same style as Whirlaway. Favored second on the boards, he settled for nothing less than first. From start to finish Jet Pilot played "catch-me" and nobody could, but it was close. Under a strong hand-ride from Eric Guerin, he outlasted Phalanx at the wire with Faultless breathing down their necks. The judges had to consult the photograph before announcing the result. It was the first photo finish in Derby history.

CITATION * May 1, 1948

Eddie Arcaro and Citation after their 1948 victory.

Warren Wright had sold his baking powder company for $28 million one year before the crash of '29 and put a large portion of it into horse racing. His wife, Lucille, had told Ben Jones when he was hired that winning the Derby was the most important thing in her life. Hiring as many as sixty employees at a time, Jones kept all his figures in his head and consulted frequently with his grooms and riders. As a result, they didn't stray. The Calumet string was divided between Jones and his son Jimmy, and they cleaned up races on both coasts as well as the Midwest. Keeping up with the Jones boys was nearly impossible.

Not since the great Man o' War had the racing establishment had a champion of the caliber of Citation, by Bull Lea. Arcaro would say he was the best horse he ever rode, though Whirlaway was more exciting. Calm, cool, and collected Citation ran with a frictionless stride, often glancing at scenery when he was on the lead. With a fine head and intelligent eye he was so uncomplicated a "Chinaman could train him," according to Ben Jones. In February 1948 Ben Jones had cut loose on the racing world another sensation—Coaltown, who many thought might best Citation with Arcaro in the Derby. Eddie had made the wrong choice before, riding Greentree's Devil Diver instead of Shut Out in 1942. When he asked Jones if he were on the right horse he was told that if Coaltown could win he'd be on him. Calumet's entry of Citation and Coaltown in the seventy-fourth Derby was so awesome that only four other stables bothered to enter. Citation, the favorite, had opened in the winter book at odds of 8 to 5 that dropped to 4 to 5 before Derby Week. The other horses in the race were there in hopes Citation and Coaltown would bump into each other and fall down.

Coaltown led in the mud the backstretch. Arcaro clucked to Cy at the quarter pole and he breezed home 3½ lengths ahead—with ears up. Citation won the Preakness and Belmont just as casually and 19 of 20 races at three for $865,000 in lifetime earnings. But Warren Wright wanted the $1 million mark and Cy complied, despite tendon trouble. He became the first equine millionaire a year after Wright's death.

© BRYANT '83

Away slowly from the gate, Steve Brooks on Ponder artfully picks up horses on the backstretch
in the inevitable devil's red and blue hoops of Calumet.

This was the Derby's Diamond Jubilee—or seventy-fifth year. Ponder would be the fourth of Calumet's eight Derby winners. With 3 seconds, 1 third, and 2 fourths in 17 starts, no other racing stable would come close. Col. E. R. Bradley with half as many winners was the nearest contender.

Ponder was one of the few Calumet starters Ben Jones had little hopes for, saying that he would be content with a piece of the purse. But Ponder had won the Derby Trial against many of the same horses the Tuesday before, which should have been some indication of his capabilities. The son of Pensive (Derby, 1944), Ponder would surprise them all as his sire had done, and run the course in exactly the same time (2:04⅕).

The outstanding favorite was Fred Hooper's Olympia with Eddie Arcaro in the saddle. Ben Jones had said nothing in the race could come close to Olympia, especially his "poor l'il ol' horse." Whether or not he was playing possum we'll never know, but Ponder won on May 7, paid $34 on a $2 bet and made fools of the experts.

As predicted, Olympia bolted to the front with Capot close behind. Palestinian had worked his way up to third. Ponder, off to a late start, was catching horses on the outside on his way to the leaders. At the far turn he was sixth and coming hard. Then in the stretch he weakened, fell back to fourth, but collected himself and came on again flying up to challenge Capot and Palestinian. As they came down to the wire, it was Ponder all alone and 3 lengths in front.

"Plain Ben" was one of the few people surprised to find himself back in the winner's circle. His unplanned win had set a trainer's Derby record—five—exceeding "Derby Dick" Thompson's score by one.

Middleground as he was at age three. Trainer Maximilian Justice Hirsch.

Col. Matt J. Winn, architect of the Derby as we know it, died before the race. He had seen every Derby, from 1875 to 1949 and had served as its guiding force since 1902, when he and some investors bought the failing track. He was succeeded by Bill Corum.

Fifteen of the country's best three-year-olds stood in the gate, with Your Host, Hill Prince, Oil Capitol, Middleground, Mr. Trouble, and Sunglow the six top contenders. At the jarring bell, W. M. Goetz's Your Host, the favorite with Johnny Longden up, took the lead over the fast track as expected—he was "unratable." On the far turn it was still Your Host now followed by Middleground who was never far back and catching up fast. At the top of the stretch, Your Host faded badly and Middleground took command. Hill Prince, who had been crowded in the far turn, ran gamely but was interfered with again by the tiring Your Host. He cleared him and still came on but couldn't catch Middleground, who flew under the wire 1½ lengths ahead of his pursuer.

Max Hirsch had himself a third Derby win. He said of Middleground's win over Hill Prince that it gave him the most pleasure of the three, as everyone likes to win when he isn't supposed to. He had taken a gamble, releasing Arcaro from his horse so that he could ride Hill Prince, and had given the ride to his young apprentice, Billy Boland. Boland rode a great race. Middleground won the Belmont and came second in the Preakness.

Until his death in 1969 at the age of 89, Hirsch was still rising at dawn in the cottage next to Barn I at Belmont to oversee the King Ranch horses as he had done for fifty years. As a boy in Texas he could recall "unfriendly Indians." At ten he went to work for John Morris riding quarter horses and then stowed away on a freight car bound for Morris's thoroughbred farm in Maryland.

Conn McCreary is jubilant on Count Turf, who strikes a handsome stance in the winner's circle.
Assistant trainer "Slim" Sully holds the reins with owner "Big Jack" Amiel just behind his arm.

The night before Derby 1951 Jack Amiel and his jockey, Conn McCreary, walked into the same restaurant where Eddie Arcaro was dining. Arcaro had the ride on the favorite, Cain Hoy Stable's Battle Morn. Amiel's horse, Count Turf, had suffered the indignation of being lumped in with "the field." Arcaro asked Amiel who he liked for the race and Amiel responded, "Are you kidding? I like my horse." "You're nuts," said Arcaro and went back to his steak.

Trainer Sol Rutchick stayed in New York. And when he learned McCreary was going to ride, offered to at least get Amiel a good jockey. McCreary had been on a losing streak since his win on Pensive (Derby, 1944), but he had risen to fame as a come-from-behind rider and Count Turf was a come-from-behind kind of horse.

Count Turf arrived by airplane in Louisville, the first Derby horse to do so. Amiel, who operated the Turf Restaurant on Broadway, was not what you would call a qualified trainer, but he would stand near trainers like Max Hirsch at the Downs in the morning, and if Hirsch sent Sonic 5 furlongs in a certain time, Amiel would instruct McCreary to do the same. McCreary exchanged the Count's chain bit for a simple D ring snaffle, and the horse ran "like a hoop around a barrel."

The Count broke with the first flight and was near the top as they passed the stands. On the backstretch Calumet's Fanfare moved toward the leaders and The Count went with him. At the far turn, McCreary had lost Fanfare and moved on the leader, Repetoire. One of the other jockeys later said, "He sounded like a can opener cutting through the field, clucking and hollering as he picked up holes and shifted his horse back and forth." Count Turf circled Repetoire on the final turn and high-tailed it for home. Royal Mustang made a bid for him but just couldn't keep up. "He just galloped," said Amiel. "He win it all by himself."

*The "Jones Boys"—the inscrutable Ben on the left and son Jimmy on the right—lead Eddie Arcaro
on Hill Gail into the 1952 Derby winner's circle.*

Hill Gail was highstrung like Blenheim II, his dam's sire, and his dam was "a well-authenticated bitch," in the words of Ben Jones, but like his uncle, Whirlaway, he could run like the wind. When Hill Gail became neurotic in the paddock before the race, Ben Jones punched him in the nose. Hill Gail was by Bull Lea, that great Calumet sire who was unplaced in the 1938 Derby but sired Derby winners Citation (1848) and Iron Liege (1957), as well as Coaltown, who was second to Citation.

Jones and Arcaro were together again and the pair would prove unbeatable. The bettors made them the overwhelming favorite at even money over White Oak Stable's Blue Man with Conn McCreary looking for a third win. When the gate opened, Hill Gail got the jump on the field. Hannibal made a bid for him on the first turn but fell away. After that nobody came close. All alone on the backstretch Arcaro sensed that Hill Gail was going to try to duck into the gap for the barn area and he smacked him with his whip. Hill Gail nearly ran away with him. He opened up a 6-length lead and outlasted Sub Fleet in a thrilling finish.

Hill Gail's winning time of 2:03⅗ came within ⅕ of a second of Whirlaway's record. It was the sixth win for Ben Jones, putting him at the top of the trainers' list over "Derby Dick" Thompson by two, and further out of reach. It was the fifth win for Arcaro, making him the winningest Derby jockey by two over Isaac Murphy and Earl Sande, and it was the fifth as well for Calumet Farm.

DARK STAR * May 2, 1953

Eric Guerin in Alfred Vanderbilt's silks on Native Dancer battles for the lead in the stretch with Dark Star.

There was no question in anybody's mind who the winner of the seventy-ninth Kentucky Derby would be—Native Dancer, Alfred G. Vanderbilt's sensational "Gray Ghost," who had won all his races leading up to the Derby. In 1952, Native Dancer had been proclaimed one of the best two-year-olds of all time, and he was the first of racing's television stars as his three-year career spanned the early years of that industry's growth. After his defeat in the Derby, he won each time out for the remainder of that season and the next. He probably would have won the Derby had he not been bumped in the early going by Money Broker. His reputation has suffered from the stigma of having not won the Derby, the significance of which, in this case, was overrated.

In all fairness to Dark Star, Harry F. Guggenheim's handsome brown colt who had won the Derby Trial, that horse ran a magnificent race. Going to the front in the first quarter, Dark Star never relinquished the lead. Correspondent, with Eddie Arcaro, recovered from an early interference and was closest to Dark Star off the far turn but had nothing left for the drive. Native Dancer had recovered under the expert handling of Eric Guerin, who had brought him up to third at the top of the stretch and, passing Correspondent, closed the gap to Dark Star. Hank Moreno went to the whip on the leader and the two horses battled down to the wire. With Native Dancer still gaining and his nose at Dark Star's cheek, they passed the finish.

Alfred Gwynne Vanderbilt struggled through two levels of crowded grandstand and must have run to be the first to congratulate his friend Harry Guggenheim on his win. The two men, though separated by twelve years in age, each represented pinnacles of wealth, social position, and sportsmanship in America. Vanderbilt shook his hand and said, "If it had to be anybody, Harry, I'm glad it was you." Native Dancer went on to win, in all, 21 races out of 22 starts, the lone blemish being the 1953 Kentucky Derby.

Determine stretches to touch the nose of Gloire Fille; they were sire and dam respectively of 1962 Derby winner, Decidedly.

This Derby was similar to that of the year before in several ways. In 1953 the gray colt, Native Dancer, was bumped in the early going and should have won but didn't. In 1954, the gray colt, Determine, was also bumped in the early going, and shouldn't have won but did. Determine became the first gray horse to win the Kentucky Derby and the first California horse to do so since Morvich in 1922. Although bred in Kentucky, Determine was owned by Californian A. J. Crevolin and campaigned in that state.

Seventeen horses went to the post for this eightieth running of the classic, with Correlation favored and Bill Shoemaker in the irons looking for his first of what would be 5 Derby wins. Arcaro, on Goyamo, was looking for his sixth. The winner of the Derby Trial, Hasty Road, with Adams up, figured to be at the top. Determine, by Alibhai out of Koubis, was a minute 870 pounds, but what he lacked in size he made up for in heart.

As the horses broke from the gate, the 5 to 1 shot, Hasty Road, crossed in front of five horses to bump Timely Tip, who jostled Determine. Though badly roughed, Determine recovered well under young Ray York, who kept him off Hasty Road's blistering pace, knowing from the Derby Trial that Hasty Road would burn them out. At the end of the mile, Hasty Road was still on top, but York had moved Determine up to challenge, passing Timely Tip. Determine responded to York's urging at the top of the stretch and passed the tiring Hasty Road. It was all over but the shouting, and there was plenty of that as all the Californians in the place sang and yelled, "California, here I come!" The little gray colt won the country's biggest race by 1½ lengths.

A portrait of Swaps at stud at John Galbreath's Darby Dan Farm (formerly Bradley's Idle Hour) in Lexington, Kentucky.

Since Swaps, one of the favorites, was owned and trained by Mormons, the church would receive 10 percent of his earnings. His owners were the Ellsworth Brothers, Rex and Reed, nondrinking Mormon cowpokes who, with $850 in savings from their $50-a-week jobs, rented an old truck and headed for the 1933 Fasig-Tipton Sales in Lexington. There they bought six mares and two weanlings for $600. From this meager stake, Rex became a power in California racing, and in 1946 borrowed $160,000 to buy the stallion, Khaled, from Aly Khan. Khaled sired a dozen stakes winners, one of which was Swaps, who failed to catch much notice at two, although he won 3 of his 6 starts, but drew attention in the early part of his next season by wins in the San Vicente Stakes and Santa Anita Derby.

Ellsworth shipped Swaps to Louisville by rail with trainer Mesach Tenney in the same boxcar. At the Downs, Tenney set up residence in Swaps's stall just as Maj. Barak Thomas had done to protect his favorite, Himyar, the night before the fourth Derby (1878).

On Derby Day, 1955, Swaps and his rider, Willie Shoemaker, had only one real rival—Nashua, with Eddie Arcaro aboard. Swaps quickly got out on the lead, and though Nashua narrowed it to a half length by the stretch, at the wire it was Swaps, clearly the best by 1½ lengths, and 8 lengths in front of Summer Tan.

Swaps returned to his home state and picked up several important stakes. But Nashua got his revenge in their match race at the end of the summer, getting off to a quick lead that Swaps was never able to overcome. John Galbreath paid Ellsworth $1 million for half-interest in Swaps when the colt finished racing, and a year later his wife put up another $1 million to buy him outright for stud duty at Darby Dan.

Needles winning the Flamingo Stakes. Needles was the first Florida Bred to win the Kentucky Derby.

Named Needles because of all the injections he was given to cure his many ailments, the bay foal grew up to win blue ribbons for his conformation as a yearling. He was speedy and precocious at two, setting a track record for 4½ furlongs as early in the year as April. At three, he began to develop the running style of his father, Ponder, winner of the 1949 Derby. He would wait until the last possible moment in a race before making his move.

In this fashion, Needles clicked off impressive scores in the Flamingo Stakes and the Florida Derby. But he was a big question mark for the Kentucky Derby. It had been six weeks since the colt had had a race or even a decent workout. Then he drew the inside post position, a disadvantage for a stretch runner. His trainer, one-time flying ace Hugh Fontaine, viewed the post position philosophically: "I love it," he said. "I might as well love it, 'cause it's the only one I'm going to get."

Needles was 27 lengths back with a half-mile to go and 15 lengths back when the pack reached "Heartbreak Lane." "When I asked him for it, he just went 'boom,'" said the jubilant Dave Erb. "We found an opening at about the three-eighths pole, went outside first, and then in." Weaving through the crowd, Needles had come back for one of the most exciting Derbies ever, but was also the slowest winner since his sire, Ponder, sauntered under the wire.

The Kentucky Derby had another "triple": Reigh Count had sired Count Fleet, who sired Count Turf. Pensive sired Ponder, who sired Needles.

Bill Shoemaker on Gallant Man, thinking he had crossed the wire, stands up briefly—giving Bill Hartack on Iron Liege the edge at the wire in the "Bad Dream" Derby.

Iron Liege was a third stringer for Calumet. Their hottest prospect, Barbizon, was two-year-old champion but developed a respiratory condition. So trainer Jimmy Jones trotted out General Duke and Iron Liege as his one-two combination. They finished one and three in the Everglades, and two and three in the Flamingo, and one and three in the Florida Derby, and one and two in the Fountain of Youth.

For the eighty-third running the smallish field included Bold Ruler, fresh from a track-record performance in the Wood, and the horse he had just nosed out in that race, Gallant Man. The good horse Round Table loomed a sharp foe.

Iron Liege pressed the pace and had his head in front as the field rolled into the stretch. Gallant Man was third, and Shoemaker was driving him. That colt overtook Iron Liege for a moment well up the stretch; however, it was not as far up the stretch as Shoemaker thought. He stood up in the irons, believing that the race was over and he had won. He realized his mistake, but not quickly enough. Bill Hartack shot Iron Liege through to the slimmest kind of victory, the first of 5 Derby victories for Hartack.

Gallant Man's owner, Ralph Lowe, had dreamed a few nights earlier that "The Shoe" would misjudge the finish. He warned trainer John Nerud and Shoemaker at dinner and perhaps as a testimony to the power of suggestion that's just what Shoemaker did.

Tim Tam at stud, with the Calumet barn in the background, looks out alertly. (insert) *Mrs. Gene Markey, the owner of Calumet.*

Calumet had developed a rising star in a horse named Kentucky Pride, but when that horse was injured they pulled Tim Tam off the bench. Tim Tam, by Tom Fool, won the Everglades, the Flamingo, the Fountain of Youth, and the Florida Derby. He then came north to Keeneland and sped 7 panels in track-record time. His final tune-up was in the Derby Trial, which he won in handy fashion.

Tim Tam had beat off a 75 to 1 shot named Lincoln Road in the Florida Derby and had been moved up into first place in the Flamingo on the disqualification of Jewel's Reward. Besides those two horses, Tim Tam also faced Silky Sullivan in the Derby, the California crowd pleaser whose come-from-behind runs were the stuff of legends.

On Derby Day the crowd had installed Jewel's Reward as the slight favorite over Tim Tam and Silky Sullivan. Silky, who had won races after having trailed by as many as 25 lengths, couldn't handle a muddy track, and Jewel's Reward ended up running an even race for fourth. The real contest was between Tim Tam and Lincoln Road. Lincoln Road led the entire race, except for the last few critical yards. Tim Tam, ranging out from the middle of the pack, under a long consistent drive, wore down his game rival for a half-length victory.

Tim Tam and his jockey, Ismael Valenzuela, scored a more decisive victory over Lincoln Road in the Preakness. Then in the Belmont he shattered a sesamoid bone at the quarter pole, yet still managed to hold on for second place. But his career was over. He would have been Calumet's third Triple Crown winner.

Tomy Lee, with Bill Shoemaker, gets a lead from trainer Frank Childs.

Texas oilman Fred Turner, Jr., figuring that somebody had already named a horse "Tommy Lee," came up with his own novel spelling. Tomy Lee was bred in England and purchased by Turner as an afterthought. He had just spent $25,000 on a fashionably bred colt and wanted the horse to have a companion for the long trek to the States. So he picked up Tomy Lee for $6,762. His high-priced colt earned back half his sales tag before an injury brought on retirement. Tomy Lee was to go on to repay his purchase price sixty times over.

At two, Tomy won 6 tries in California, then traveled east to lose 2 tough contests to First Landing. At three he came up short in his early West Coast starts, but was undefeated in the East. The striking-looking colt came up to the Derby with two impressive victories at Keeneland: a track record for 7 in the first furlongs and then the Blue Grass Stakes. In the Derby, his old rival, First Landing, went off as the slight favorite.

Tomy Lee, with Willie Shoemaker in the irons, put in a tough fight to gain the lead, but then having done so he succumbed to Sword Dancer with a quarter of a mile to go. As they rounded the turn for home, Tomy Lee, along the rail, drew even but carried Sword Dancer wide on the turn. As they battled through the stretch, Sword Dancer lugged back in but just failed to outlast Tomy Lee. Sword Dancer's jockey claimed foul but it was disallowed by the stewards. In this his second Derby win, "Shoe" made up for his ride in the "Bad Dream" Derby.

Tomy Lee was retired at the end of the year but had difficulty getting mares in foal, so at six he was sent back to the track. He picked up four more winner's checks before resuming the life of leisure as a stallion.

Venetian Way jogs out onto the foggy track for an early morning gallop.

The damp crowd of 75,000 fancied Tompion, at practically even money, due to a four-race record that included the Santa Anita Derby and the Blue Grass Stakes. Also popular at the pari-mutuels was Bally Ache, who had defeated the third favorite, Venetian Way, in three out of four of their encounters, including a 7-furlong prep at Churchill Downs several days before the Derby.

In the eighty-sixth running, Venetian Way was third after 5 furlongs, second with a quarter mile to go, first at the top of the stretch, and first where it counted the most. His time of 2:02 ⅖ was the fastest Derby run on an "off" track. Sports writer Red Smith compared the track condition that day to "used eating tobacco."

Especially warmed by the victory of this game colt were its owner, Isaac Blumberg, and trainer, Vic Sovinski. They had campaigned the good colt, Lincoln Road, in 1958, but kept running into Tim Tam. Said Sovinski, "I would rather win the Kentucky Derby than any other race in the world, and I don't care if I never win another race." This was the second of five Derby wins for jockey Bill Hartack.

Carry Back and jockey John Sellers, in the blue and silver silks of Mrs. Katherine Price, at the sixteenth pole.

Horses that perfect a late rush that gets them to the wire just in time tend to be big favorites with the public. Fans are also taken with honest, hard-knocking horses. The public also likes a Cinderella story, where a bargain-basement horse rises up to beat his better-bred rivals. Carry Back was a born crowd pleaser.

His owner-trainer, Jack Price, was a new breed of horseman and his colt came from Ocala, a new center of the thoroughbred breeding industry in central Florida. The horse that Jack Price bred for a $400 stud fee to a nonwinning mare bought for $265 raced a grueling 21 times as a freshman. Carry Back set a couple of track records that year and came from off the pace to win such important fixtures as the Cowdin, the Garden State, and the Remsen.

Carry Back developed into the people's horse through his stirring contests with Crozier in the rich Florida winter stakes. On Derby Day, the betting public took a good look at Crozier, who had just sped to a Churchill Downs track record earlier that week in the Derby Trial. But they made Carry Back the favorite, his support coming largely from the $2 bets of the infield multitudes.

Carry Back gave the fans just what they had packed the Downs to see. At the quarter pole he was 13 lengths back, but coming into the stretch he was fourth, trailing Crozier by 6 lengths. Then John Sellers let him all the way out and it was all over for the speedy Crozier as Carry Back drove fans wild with an almost 2-length win.

Carry Back won the Preakness, but was upset in the Belmont. He'd be back to battle the best of his era, though, for years to come, and a career total of $1,226,665. He was racing's second millionaire, the first since Citation.

The beautiful head of Decidedly with trainer Horatio Luro.

On the basis of his record, Decidedly had little going for him, but he was the son of 1954 Derby winner Determine; in addition he was bred by Californian George Pope, Jr., of the noted El Peco Ranch, trained by Argentinian Horatio Luro, and ridden by Bill Hartack.

The *Blood-Horse* filed this report on the 1962 Derby: "It was not only the fastest Derby in the race's 88-year history, it was one of the most exciting. The time of 2:00⅖ was a full second better than Whirlaway's record which had stood since 1941. During the hectic mile and a quarter, the lead changed from the outsider Lee Town to Sunrise Country to Admiral's Voyage to Roman Line before the gray Decidedly found an opening to the outside at the eighth pole. From then on, with Bill Hartack riding hard, the gray moved 2¼ lengths clear of the surprising Roman Line." Decidedly was the second gray to win the classic. The first was his sire, Determine.

For Hartack, it was Derby win number three. He was the Bobby Fischer of racing, blunt to the point of rudeness. Born in poverty and the son of a coal miner, he'd worked his way to the top by tooth and nail. "Hatred is necessary for my work," he once explained to a reporter. "The madder I get, the better I ride." Tying Eddie Arcaro's record with five wins, it took Arcaro twenty-one tries while Hartack did it in nine. The best riding average still is Winkfield's, with his two wins, one second, and one third in four attempts.

A thorn from the rose blanket jabs Chateaugay, who never needed an excuse to "act up." Braulio Baeza sits coolly, and owner John Galbreath, left, holds the roses.

The mint julep is the Derby's official drink, and julep toasts were being drunk to the expected Derby winner long before the race was run and were still being drunk to a son of Swaps named Chateaugay long after the last race was over.

Chateaugay had looked sharp winning the Blue Grass Stakes a few weeks earlier, but the crowd had two undefeated horses to consider, so this sleek chestnut paid a respectable $20.80 to his backers. Jockey Braulio Baeza, the Panamanian sensation, timed his charge perfectly from the middle of the pack and wore down the tiring leaders. It was the first Derby win for owner-breeder John W. Galbreath, trainer J. P. Conway, and Baeza.

Chateaugay carried a little good luck with him in the race. Galbreath's cook sent along a few chicken wishbones, and the millionaire owner dutifully fastened them to his horse's tack before sending Chateaugay out to victory.

Canadian owner E. P. Taylor holds Northern Dancer with Bill Hartack up. Trainer Horatio Luro is on the left of Taylor.

As the field rounded the stretch for home, the second favorite, Northern Dancer, was still in the lead after clocking swift fractions with Bill Hartack in the irons. Moving quickly through the pack was the favored Hill Rise with Shoemaker aboard. Hill Rise was in the process of running the fastest final quarter mile in Derby history as he pulled even with the leader. But the race was probably won when Hartack moved decisively with Northern Dancer at the 5-furlong pole, taking Shoemaker and Hill Rise by surprise. The two horses had been running side by side behind a wall of three horses. Hartack eased his horse away from the rail and Northern Dancer spurted in front of Hill Rise and to the outside. Shoemaker later said that he could not get his big horse moving in time to prevent Northern Dancer's nimble escape.

Northern Dancer edged the favored Hill Rise in the record time of 2:00 flat. His Derby win was the first for a Canadian bred and for breeder E. P. Taylor. It was the second time around for trainer Horatio Luro, whose Decidedly had smashed all previous Derby records in 1962 and now broke that time by ⅖ of a second with Northern Dancer.

Northern Dancer won four stakes as a three-year-old—the Flamingo, Florida Derby, and Blue Grass—on his way to Churchill Downs. After running for the roses, he picked up the black-eyed Susans of the Preakness and then won the most important Canadian classic, the Queen's Plate. He is best known for his success as a sire and for the astronomical prices his yearlings fetch.

All alone in midstretch, though they would be challenged imminently, are Lucky Debonair and Bill Shoemaker in Ada L. Rice's colors.

Frank Catrone, a short, portly man, was one of a few trainers to face the 4′ 11″ Bill Shoemaker on even terms. Lucky Debonair, the Vertex colt out of a Count Fleet mare, had won the Santa Anita Derby and the Blue Grass Stakes at 1⅛ miles (the perfect "prep" distance to the Derby) by slim margins. No one realized that, once on the lead, Lucky Debonair would try to pull himself up. He always had energy to spare, but Tom Rolfe and Bold Lad were favored for this Derby.

Flag Raiser took the lead past the stands, with Lucky Debonair 2 lengths back. Johnny Rotz on Native Charger thought he was sitting "in the golden chair" coming up the backstretch behind Flag Raiser with Bold Lad sixth and

Dapper Dan dead last. Flag Raiser, still on the lead coming out of the far turn started to tire, and Lucky Debonair took command. Ron Turcotte, in his first Derby appearance, on Tom Rolfe, tried to slip through on the rail inside Flag Raiser, but Bobby Ussery closed them off. In midstretch Lucky Debonair was all alone and could have coasted, but then came Dapper Dan from last place to challenge him in the final dash. A chestnut son of Ribot, Dapper Dan had looped the field and was still gaining on the leader when they passed under the wire with Lucky Debonair clinging to his lead by a neck. Tom Rolfe was third and Bold Lad, the victim of leg problems, beat only one horse of the eleven.

KAUAI KING * May 7, 1966

Groom "Popeye" Stevenson leads the son of Native Dancer in a victory procession from the winner's circle of the 92nd Kentucky Derby. "It's the biggest day of my life!" exclaimed Popeye.

On a warm and "fast-track" day, the son of Native Dancer, who was unbeaten in 22 starts except the Derby, avenged his father's defeat of 1953 and did it leading from wire to wire. Though slightly favored, the colors were unfamiliar to the crowd of over 100,000, as was the jockey, Donald Brumfield. Brumfield was one of the best at rating a horse on the lead and was known in Louisville, where he had raced over the Churchill Downs oval hundreds of times.

It had all the appearances of being a boring Derby. Overshadowed by the absence of Graustark, who was injured, the fifteen remaining horses seemed to be the leftovers of what had been a good crop of three-year-olds. No one expected the thrilling race it became, least of all Kauai King's owner, Mike Ford, who had only been in the racing game six years. But he and trainer Henry Forrest believed in the colt they had brought along: Kauai King had won 6 of his last 8 times out.

No one else in the classic ever really had a chance. At the bell, Kauai King broke so well from the gate he was on top by the first turn and, neatly cutting across the field, took the lead on the inside rail. They sizzled the first quarter in :22⅘. When they covered the mile in 1:35 with the field backed up ominously behind them, it looked like it was all over for the King. Horses just don't do a mile in the Derby in that time and still hang on to win. John Sellers drove Advocator in hot pursuit, nearly catching Kauai King at the quarter pole. Abe's Hope, with Shoemaker, made a spectacular run circling the field on the turn, but faded abruptly at the top of the stretch. Stupendous attempted to come alongside with Blue Skyer, but while Blue Skyer held on to just miss the roses by a nose, Stupendous gave up the ghost.

Don Brumfield said to himself as he came down the stretch, whipping and pumping, with everyone in the race taking a shot at them, "Help me Lord, 'cause I need you now," but the veteran Kentucky jock didn't need a hand on this day that made him the "happiest hillbilly hardboot you've ever seen!"

As he tossed his whip to his groom, "Popeye," he spoke for Kauai King as well when he said to Henry Forrest, "Thank you, Papa."

A montage of Proud Clarion and jockey Bobby Ussery after their muddy win in the 93rd Derby.

Proud Clarion, John Galbreath's "second stringer," defeated the favored Damascus with a jockey who was second choice. Braulio Baeza generally rode for Galbreath's Darby Dan Farm, but his contract had run out six days before Derby time and Galbreath had understood when he wanted to ride the Phipps's Successor. Ussery had lost his mount when Reflected Glory, after a successful winter, came up with a sore shin. Galbreath remembered the terrific ride Ussery had given his Bramalea to beat Cicada in the Coaching Club Oaks of 1962 and hoped he'd repeat on Proud Clarion. And Bobby had a hunch that whatever horse he was on, this was his year. Trainer Loyd "Boo" Gentry had just missed the Derby the year before when Graustark, who would have been favored, came up lame after running in the Blue Grass on a sloppy track (he never ran again). Galbreath had hopes for Proud Clarion, who had improved remarkably, running second in the Blue Grass, but thought Damascus with his 6 wins in 8 starts the logical choice.

Ninth going past the stands the first time, Ussery and Clarion didn't pose much of a threat to anyone. Barbs Delight, the "rabbit," had the lead, with Shoemaker on Damascus sitting pretty in the fourth slot. At the half-mile, "Shoe" was like a cat waiting to spring on three mice, while Ussery began to move Proud Clarion up on the outside. By the top of the turn they were in the clear and took aim on the stretch. Shoemaker went for Barbs Delight, who had absolutely no intention of quitting, in spite of incredible fractions. Proud Clarion came alongside the two and didn't quit till he was under the wire a length to the good of Barbs Delight. The longest-priced winner since Gallahadion upset Bimelech in 1940, Proud Clarion came in at 30 to 1 in the rain. It was the third fastest Derby in history—2:00⅗.

Calumet's eighth Kentucky Derby winner, on the right with Peter Fuller's Dancer's Image, who ran first but was disqualified.

Dancer's Image came under the wire 1½ lengths ahead of Forward Pass, and Peter Fuller, with his wife Joan and their children carrying "Dancer's Image" signs, made a dash for the winner's circle. It was the most fantastic thrill of a lifetime for Fuller. For jockey Bobby Ussery, it was a double pleasure, as this win plus his triumph the year before on Proud Clarion made him the first jockey since Jimmy Winkfield (1901 and 1902) to win two Derbys back to back.

While the winners savored their victory with champagne as the guests of track president Wathen Knebelcamp, a chemist in the mobile laboratory was testing urine and saliva samples from both the winner and another horse in the race picked at random, as was the procedure for all the races. The specimens were tagged and half of each tag, with the horse's name on it, was sealed in an envelope. The lab technician, having that part of the tag with just a number on it, knew only that the tests were from any of the ten races that day. They were testing for traces of Butazolidin, a pain-killing analgesic, which was legal for use in training but outlawed during a race. One of the samples changed color. When Churchill Downs steward Lewis Finley opened the sealed envelope Monday morning and discovered the number of the tainted sample matched the tag with the Derby winner's name on it, he was shocked.

Lou Cavalaris, who trained Dancer's Image, wasn't in Louisville when Dancer's Image twisted his right front ankle "playing around." Butazolidin was administered to relieve the swelling and the pain several days before the Derby. The colt developed colic the next day, apparently from the "bute," a fact Fuller pointed to in the ensuing hearings, deducing that if Dancer's Image had been on "bute" in the Derby, he would have been sick the following day. Litigation continued for several years before the decision went to Forward Pass.

Bill Hartack sits on Majestic Prince as he is weighed before the Belmont Stakes.

The story of the ninety-fifth Derby is that of Johnny Longden and the horse he trained and exercised himself. The spectacular-looking chestnut colt by Raise a Native was unbeaten and favored to win. The ex-jockey kept him supplied with his favorite peppermint candy.

As the race got underway, Top Knight faded suddenly and was overtaken by Paul Mellon's Arts and Letters. Bill Hartack watched Arts and Letters go by, then roused "The Prince." Majestic Prince caught and passed Arts and Letters at the eighth pole, but Arts and Letters, with Braulio Baeza, hung on and dueled down to the wire with Dike, who had come from out of nowhere. All three passed under the wire together, with Majestic Prince in front by only a neck. Longden became the first man to win the Kentucky Derby both as a jockey (Count Fleet, 1943) and as a trainer. Bill Hartack tied Eddie Arcaro for the most wins of a jockey.

Majestic Prince went on to win the Preakness but after that effort was so exhausted "he jus' sleep and sleep," his groom said. Longden argued with owner Frank McMahon not to run in the Belmont. The horse had "corded up" after the Preakness, and his flanks were sunken. He had lost over 40 pounds. "Something has been said about me being a quitter," said McMahon, and he insisted that the horse run—to Longden's despair. Majestic Prince ran a game race to finish second to Arts and Letters, his old foe, and lost the Triple Crown. Then he developed leg troubles and, as Longden predicted, never ran again. The horse whose star had risen so quickly was ruined. Majestic Prince was not the first victim of the Triple Crown. Old Rosebud didn't recover for two years after the Derby, Canonero II was lame for a year after his efforts, and Dancer's Image was through after the Derby and Preakness.

Dust Commander sniffs inquisitively at Mike Manganello's bouquet of roses. A guard in the background savors his single bud.

The ninety-sixth Derby was a "blessed event" for Dust Commander and Mike Manganello. Archbishop Emmanuel Milingo of Zambia had stepped in front of the horse as he paraded in the Keeneland paddock before the Blue Grass Stakes and performed the usual blessing for domestic animals. Then he went to the window and bet $2 across the board on the little colt by Bold Commander (by Bold Ruler). The black archbishop was not there by accident, but as a guest of the owners.

The heretofore unnoticed colt Robert Lehmann had bought as a yearling for $6,500 easily trounced Corn off the Cob and the Blue Grass field and paid 35 to 1. Lehmann, who was on the border of India and Nepal tracking "big game" at the time, flew back 70 hours to see Dust Commander run in the Derby.

Archbishop Milingo couldn't be at the Derby and when Mrs. Lehmann asked if he shouldn't bless the horse again the archbishop informed her that when a horse is blessed, he is blessed; however, he did have a premonition involving a number 4 horse.

Mike Manganello was not a big-name Northern jockey, but he had ridden the Louisville track hundreds of times. So when he and Dust Commander were badly roughed up at the start, he maneuvered his nimble colt to the inside rail where they hung saving ground. At the half-mile pole he let Dust Commander start to pick up horses by himself but going into the last turn a sigh went up from the crowd: not Dust Commander but the number 4 horse, Holy Land of all names, had gone down. Diane Crump, the first woman to ride in the Derby, was not involved, but Hector Pilar lay motionless. Manganello swung Dust Commander wide in the homestretch and took the lead. Hector Pilar survived his back injuries and the archbishop of Zambia took home $1,662.60 for the Zambia Helper's Society.

CANONERO II * May 1, 1971

Owner Pedro Baptista and Canonero II after the colt's win in the 97th Derby.

On March 31, a month before the Kentucky Derby, the heavily favored Hoist the Flag broke his leg in a workout at Belmont Park. He was saved for stud duty by the genius of equine surgeon Jacques Jenny, and the Derby was wide open. The accident was devastating to owner Jane Clark and trainer Sidney Watters, of Middleburg, Virginia. But what was a tragedy for the famous horse became a Cinderella story for the unknown.

Juan Arias was raised in the slums of Caracas, Venezuela, but he attended a four-year government school for horse trainers. He was eventually put in charge of eccentric industrialist Pedro Baptista's losing string, which began to win for him consistently. Canonero began life with a foreleg that bent backward from the knee. The unsightly blemish kept buyers away, despite his Pretendre-Dixieland II breeding, and he sold for $1,200 to Venezuela. He moved like a crab, but he won his first outing by 6½ lengths. His two-year-old season tapered off, but at three he came back strong, and Baptista nominated him for the Triple Crown.

No one in the States had heard of Canonero II or knew that, at Venezuela's La Rinconanda racetrack, he won at 1¼ miles, the Derby distance, two months before the Derby, in deep sand and at an altitude of 3,000 feet. When the Canonero entourage arrived at Churchill Downs they were shunned by the racing establishment. The individualistic Arias would work his horse any time of the day, and often lead him with a rope around his neck. He was not invited to the pre-Derby dinner in honor of Derby trainers, and in the betting Canonero was lumped in with the "field" at 9 to 1.

In the paddock, the tension in Canonero's saddling stall was unbearable. Arias's hands were shaking so hard he couldn't tighten the girth without help. Robert Kleberg of King Ranch watched the unknown South American colt and commented that he was about the best-looking he'd ever seen.

Canonero got off to a bad start, fifteenth in the field of twenty. Two Calumet horses dominated the race through the far turn, but Canonero, reaching the turn eighteenth, opened up and, with Gustavo Avila whipping like a windmill, looped the field. They streaked under the wire 3½ lengths ahead of Jim French, followed by Bold Reason. Silence blanketed the grandstand. "Canonero II?" exclaimed a reporter. "Who the hell was Canonero I?"

Canonero went on to win the Preakness, and the country was his. Offered $3 million if Canonero won the Triple Crown, Baptista ran the tired colt in the Belmont against Arias's objections. He ran fourth and sold to the sagacious Kleburg for $1.5 million.

RIVA RIDGE * May 6, 1972

Penny Tweedy gives Riva Ridge a congratulatory pat in the winner's circle.

In 1936 Christopher Chenery, chairman of Southern Natural Gas Company, bought the old family homestead where Chenery had spent boyhood summers in Doswell, Virginia. The 2,600-acre "Meadow" became the nursery for 41 stakes winners, among them Hill Prince, First Landing, Cicada, Riva Ridge, and Secretariat. When Chenery was hospitalized in 1967, his daughter, Penny, took over the Meadow and, determined to keep the blue and white blocks of her father's silks flying, made it the operation it is today.

By Riva Ridge's two-year-old spring, Penny knew she had something when she wrote in her stable log, "The boys like. Will be a racehorse." Penny chose trainer Roger Laurin, son of Canadian trainer Lucien Laurin, but when Eddie Nelroy, Ogden Phipps's trainer, died in 1971, Roger went to work for him and suggested his father to Mrs. Tweedy. They hit it off immediately, and when Riva's regular jockey, Chuck Baltazar, was suspended, Lucien got the Canadian champion, Ron Turcotte, and the "team" was formed, along with Ed Sweat and Charlie Davis, groom and exercise rider for Lucien.

In Riva's two-year-old summer, Lucien Lauren sent him out to work with the four-year-old speedster, Three Martinis, to "move him up a bit." He told the boy on Three Martinis to stay back with Riva and not "break" him. As the two were flying down the track, Charlie Davis on Riva said to the other, "The man wants this horse to work. Let your horse out!" The other replied, "I can't pick him up and carry him!" It was then Lucien knew he had a superhorse. He broke the world record for $1\frac{3}{16}$ miles that year in $1:52\frac{2}{5}$ and earned over $503,000. Riva Ridge was the two-year-old champ.

After a long rest in Florida, he came up to the Derby in perfect shape mentally and physically despite his loss in the "Everglades," where he was trapped on the rail. He won the Blue Grass, and in the Derby, broke from the number 9 slot and headed straight for the lead. When Marquez, on Hold Your Peace, made a move to test him, Riva and Turcotte took a length lead. When Marquez moved up again at the far turn, Riva spurted away and led the field by 3 lengths coming into the homestretch. No Le Hace came on but could not catch him as he sped under the wire $3\frac{1}{4}$ lengths ahead. In his hospital room in New York, the immobilized Chris Chenery saw his daughter on television clutching the gold trophy. Christopher Chenery finally had his Derby.

118

Bryant '83

SECRETARIAT * May 5, 1973

Oil painting of "Big Red" coming straight on with an intensity and power unequaled in modern times.

Secretariat captured the Triple Crown in 1973, the first horse to do so since Citation twenty-five years earlier.

"Wow!" exclaimed Penny Tweedy when she first saw the chestnut foal by Bold Ruler out of Somethingroyal. When she turned her "Wow colt" over to Lucien Laurin for training, Lucien was afraid he was too good-looking to really run. Secretariat won 8 races straight as a two-year-old. Before his first start at three he was syndicated for over $6 million.

Secretariat became a TV star, the first racehorse with a Nielsen rating, and his handsome face graced the covers of *Time, Newsweek,* and *Sports Illustrated.* The day of the ninety-ninth Derby, he was powerful, aloof, and self-contained in the paddock. Starting last from the gate, as he usually preferred, he gathered steam at a steady rate. Like a locomotive, the powerful haunches collected, then propelled him forward in earth-eating strides. At the end of the clubhouse turn, he finally fired, and the red streak blasted up the backstretch, gobbling all in his way. Shecky Greene, the speed horse, was still on top with Sham, Secretariat's nemesis in the Wood Memorial, keeping him in his sights. Sham passed Shecky Greene on the last turn and, as they straightened out for the stretch, there was Secretariat alongside. It was a two-horse race. Sham, his mouth bleeding heavily from an accident in the gate, held on gamely, but could not outstay "Big Red" who was still gaining momentum. Secretariat's individual fractions were :25⅕, :24⅕, :23⅗, and :23: He ran each quarter mile faster than the one before, and beat Northern Dancer's 1964 record by ⅗ of a second. It was the second win in a row for Ron Turcotte.

Secretariat repeated his performance in the Preakness, and in the Belmont on June 9, he barged down the stretch 31 lengths ahead. He took a full 2⅗ seconds off Gallant Man's 1957 record.

Poor Riva Ridge. His own brilliant Derby victory eclipsed and his $1 million career forgotten, he turned his rump to his stall opening when the crowds gathered around Secretariat's stall next door. In the only time they ever met on the track, both Riva and his stablemate broke the world record for one and one-eighth miles in the Marlboro Cup, but Secretariat won by 3½ lengths over Riva. He was a great horse, unfortunately overshadowed by one greater.

Worth over $11 million together, the two horses were vanned to Kentucky for stud duties. The blue and white Chenery silks would be around for a long time.

CANNONADE * May 4, 1974

Trainer Woody Stephens on a lead pony takes Cannonade and Angel Cordero out for a morning spin.

It was the one hundredth year of the Kentucky Derby, a century of fine racing at the Louisville racetrack unperturbed by two world wars; even the Great Depression only delayed the Derby of '29 by a month. John Olin's Cannonade, trained by Woody Stephens and ridden by the Puerto Rican jockey Angel Cordero, won this centennial Derby in the unspectacular time of 2:05 over a fast track. What was spectacular was the event. All previous attendance records were shattered by 30,000. The winner won more money ($274,000), the bettors handed over more money ($3,444,649 on the Derby alone), and everyone in the infield had more fun than any previous year. Police were helpless to prevent the hordes from hanging on the inside rail. They were unable to chase a band of half-naked youths from the top of one of the toteboards or to catch any of the streakers who ran amok. Princess Margaret, the Queen of England's fun-loving sister, said it was a lovely day of racing in the country. She donated a special jeweled cup to the winner. More horses by one than Reigh Count's record field of twenty-three went to the post, half of which shouldn't have been there. It was a horse from the field, Hudson County, who set the pace and held on for place money.

At the end of "God Save the Queen," "The Stars and Stripes Forever," and "My Old Kentucky Home," the gates loosed a phalanx of charging, color-splashed equines. There was a lot of bumping and knocking. Shoemaker on Agitate was shaken up and trapped on the rail, but Cordero dodged and scooted Cannonade through holes all the way, catching Hudson County and leaving him by 4 lengths at the eighth pole and going on to win by the same margin. Of his video game–like ride through the traffic, Cordero said, "It was a beautiful trip."

FOOLISH PLEASURE * May 3, 1975

John Greer leads Jacinto Vasquez on Foolish Pleasure past the tulips to the winner's circle.

On May 3, Foolish Pleasure put to rest any doubts as to his true quality when he triumphed in a spectacular manner in the 101st Kentucky Derby. Seventy-seven-year-old John Greer was delighted with his check for $209,000 plus, and reminded everyone of his horse's hard-fought win in the Wood in spite of lingering foot problems from the Florida Derby.

The grandson of Bold Ruler and Tom Fool had distinguished himself as a two-year-old winning all 7 of his outings, and in this race was the third Florida bred, after Needles and Carry Back, to take the Kentucky crown jewel and trounce the only two horses that had ever beaten him—Prince Thou Art and Sylvan Place. The favored Avatar and Diabolo from the "Coast" were relegated to second and third, and Bombay Duck, who gave him a problem in the Wood, finished last.

Bombay Duck went off to a blistering lead, clocking fractions of :22 for the quarter, and the half in :45⅗. Jacinto Vasquez kept Foolish Pleasure off the pace until Bombay Duck faded on the far turn when Avatar and Master Derby took control. With a tremendous surge of speed, Foolish Pleasure drove between the two horses at the head of the stretch just in time to avoid the collision when Diabolo came in on Avatar. Avatar, knocked sideways, gamely managed to finish second. There was a steward's inquiry, but both jockeys of the California horses said that they couldn't have caught Foolish Pleasure.

Chic Anderson, announcing the stretch duel, got so excited he called Prince Thou Art in front instead of Foolish Pleasure, which sounded good to Braulio Baeza in sixth on Prince Thou Art, but did not in the least deter Vasquez, who thought, "I don't know where you are, Baeza, but I'm here at the wire winning this race."

Three months later a match race was set between Foolish Pleasure, the colt of the year, and Ruffian, the filly of the year. It was a box-office smash. This unnatural contest was viewed by millions, who were then treated to the gruesome spectacle of a fine and brilliant filly snapping a leg. Foolish Pleasure had got the jump on the black filly by a head coming out of the gate, but she had rallied and was leading him halfway up the backstretch. The crowd held its collective breath. They were going too fast. Then Ruffian bobbled, ran on her broken hind leg for a few strides, and stopped. All efforts to save her were unsuccessful and she was buried in the infield of Belmont Park.

BOLD FORBES * May 1, 1976

Angel Cordero on Bold Forbes is led into the winner's circle by trainer Lazaro Barrera.

It's a long way from the backstretch of El Commandante Racetrack in Puerto Rico to the finish line of the Kentucky Derby, but that's where winning horse and rider got their starts. Completing the Latin American lock on the 1976 Derby was the trainer who saddled his first winner at Oriental Park in Havana, Cuba.

Angel Cordero was born on the racetrack. Both grandfathers were jockeys and his father, Angel Cordero, Sr., was probably the greatest rider from Puerto Rico—until Junior came along. The younger Cordero picked up three months' worth of suspensions his first year, but he still was the year's top rider at El Commandante.

Bold Forbes was bred in the blue grass but was sent to Puerto Rico to be broken and trained by the Ubarris, the island's first family of the thoroughbred sport. He was quick to outclass his competition there and he was shipped back to the States where he won a couple of freshman stakes on the tough New York circuit. At three he tuned up with a stakes win in a sprint, thought to be his best distance. He then successfully stretched out to a mile and an eighth in the Wood.

Bold Forbes was trained by Hall of Fame trainer Laz Barrera, one of the many Cuban Barrera Brothers and sons successfully plying the training trade at American tracks. He took the speedy grandson of Bold Ruler to Kentucky to face the heavily favored Honest Pleasure in the 102nd running of the Derby. Cordero drove "the Puerto Rican Cadillac" to a dramatic upset victory by using his colt's speed to get to the front, and there he stayed, putting away a fierce challenge from Honest Pleasure. Sometime after this his second Derby victory, Cordero returned to Puerto Rico and placed the blanket of roses on his father's grave.

Bold Forbes and Honest Pleasure hooked in a speed duel in the Preakness that burned them both out. In the Belmont Bold Forbes did what no sprinter should be able to do—last a mile and a half. Cordero got the colt out so far and so fast that he was able to hold on for the win, even though he practically crawled across the finish line. Bold Forbes was named the three-year-old champion of 1976, and helped his trainer earn an Eclipse Award.

SEATTLE SLEW * May 7, 1977

Oil painting of Seattle Slew beating Run Dusty Run and Sanhedrin in the stretch of the 1977 Derby.

"Well above average in size, shiny coat, bright, alert . . . a well-developed shoulder . . . a good spring of ribs (lots of room for heart and lungs) . . . out in the right foreleg . . . free of worms." That was the auction company's modest assessment of Seattle Slew. The bidding started at $3,000 and 90 seconds later the gavel came down at $17,000. Slew was bought by Mickey Taylor, a Washington lumberman, who took the advice of veterinarian Dr. Jim Hill to bid for Seattle Slew. Hill and his wife became partners with Taylor and his wife in Slew and a handful of other horses. A gawky colt, Slew soon picked up the nickname Baby Huey, after the cartoon character who is always doing everything wrong. But his trainer, Billy Turner, an ex-steeplechase rider, took his time with the colt, not starting him till September of his freshman season. Seattle Slew's 3 consecutive wins that year included the Champagne Stakes, and it was enough to land him the two-year-old championship. At three, Seattle Slew took major Derby preps in the North and South—the Flamingo Stakes and the Wood Memorial.

The "Slew Crew" of nine—the Taylors, the Hills, the Turners, and assorted friends all arrived in one car on Derby Day. "Huey has all the dignity and the rest of us come up short," said Mrs. Turner. Slew, piloted by the veteran French jockey, Jean Cruget, overcame a bumpy start and was rushed into contention. Squeezing through the pack he dueled with For a Moment for the lead and then put them all away with a quarter mile left to run.

The Kentucky Derby was step number one in Seattle Slew's trip to the Triple Crown. He was the first undefeated horse to do so. Slew was also named both three-year-old champion and horse of the year in 1977, and top handicap horse in 1978.

AFFIRMED * May 6, 1978

*Affirmed looks nonchalant in the winner's circle of the 1978 Kentucky Derby. Eighteen-year-old
"Stevie" Cauthen grins in this double oil portrait.*

The 104th Kentucky Derby had all the ingredients of a great contest. There was the East versus the West. It had age and tradition versus youth and progress. Both favorites had met before and each had beaten the other.

On one hand, there was Calumet Farm's outstanding colt, Alydar, the son of Raise a Native. Alydar was the first outstanding Derby prospect for Calumet since Forward Pass's victory ten years earlier. On the other side was Harbor View Farm's Affirmed, a chestnut colt by Exclusive Native. Both these horses had won their last four races with impressive showings. They had met before as two-year-olds and were split, 4 wins for Affirmed and 2 for Alydar. On Derby Day, Alydar went off as the 6 to 5 favorite—the odds on Affirmed were 9 to 5.

The race was an exciting, classic duel between two brilliant colts. After the break, Affirmed running easily kept with the leaders for the first mile.

Alydar was held back, but started to move up at the mile. As the leaders hit the stretch it was Affirmed first, Believe It second, and a fast-closing Alydar third. At the wire it was Affirmed by 1½ lengths over Alydar second, and Believe It third.

Affirmed went on to win both the Preakness and the Belmont to become American racing's tenth Triple Crown winner, the third in a short five-year span that began with Secretariat in 1973, continued with Seattle Slew in 1977, and ended with Affirmed in 1978. They were the superstars of the seventies. It should not be omitted that Affirmed also helped focus the national spotlight on Steve Cauthen, the eighteen-year-old Kentucky boy, who piloted Affirmed so brilliantly. The jockey Laz Barrera said probably didn't come from Kentucky at all but from a spaceship had the wisdom of the ages, the finesse of Arcaro, and the hands of Shoemaker.

SPECTACULAR BID   *   May 5, 1979

In this oil painting Spectacular Bid avenges his loss to Coastal in the Belmont Stakes by beating him in the Marlboro Cup.

The 1979 Kentucky Derby had been touted as a contest between Flying Paster and Spectacular Bid, both highly regarded horses on winning streaks. The difference would be told, it was thought, by the greater experience of forty-two-year-old Donald Pierce on Flying Paster. The pressure on Spectacular Bid's teen-age jockey, Ronnie Franklin, was almost unbearable. Wisely, trainer Bud Delp helped get him a ride on Seethreepeo in the $25,000 Twin Spires, the race immediately preceding the Derby, which they won.

As the gates opened for the Derby, Spectacular Bid stalled and the crowd prepared to blame Franklin. Two days before the race rain had deluged Churchill Downs. The dirt packed in the horses' hooves and the clods thrown back discouraged the best of them. Flying Paster, the second favorite, appeared to scramble, and Screen King, the third favorite, seemed to jump up and down. Ronnie took his big gray horse wide around the pack and it was clear sailing to the wire.

It was "Bid's" eleventh straight victory for owners Harry and Teresa Meyerhoff and a vindication for Franklin, who would ride him again on his home ground, Pimlico Race Track, in the Preakness and triumph one more time. Still the doubters encouraged Bud Delp to take Franklin off Spectacular Bid for the Belmont Stakes, third leg of the Triple Crown. Delp refused, keeping faith in the young jockey who was like a son to him. In the Belmont, Bid went straight to the front, uncharacteristically, as if under instructions to set a record. William Haggin Perry's Coastal, who had been campaigned lightly and probably saved for this occasion, wore down the Kentucky Derby winner and won.

Although Bid came out of the race sore, and a stray bandage pin that had stuck in his foot the day of the race was blamed for his defeat, Franklin was removed for the Spectacular Bid–Coastal rematch in the Marlboro Cup. Bid won it handily with the veteran Bill Shoemaker aboard.

GENUINE RISK * May 3, 1980

An oil portrait of Genuine Risk in the stretch of the 106th Kentucky Derby.

Not since Harry Payne Whitney's Regret in 1915 had a filly won the Kentucky Derby.

Genuine Risk was undefeated going into the Wood Memorial, the important prep race six weeks before the Derby; however, in this her first try against the colts, she'd finished third to Plugged Nickle, a Derby candidate, in a slow time. The mare was listless and off her feed after the race. Sixteen-year-old Mathew Firestone, who had selected Genuine Risk at the Fasig-Tipton sales, was discouraged. The Derby distance so early in the year is stressful for colts and much more so for the slightly-built fillies, a reason they are given a 5-pound weight allowance at that time. Although fillies have won many of France's great classic, the Arc de Triomphe, this is run in October of their third year. Genuine Risk was slight even for a filly.

Genuine Risk was not entered in the Blue Grass Stakes, the final Derby prep, but stepped out onto the track that morning for her first time since the Wood. Jacinto Vasquez said she nearly pulled his arms out. Trainer Leroy Jolley later watched the Blue Grass, and when Rockhill Native won in roughly the same slow time Plugged Nickle had the Wood, and Prince Valiant, who had figured strongly, straggled home last, he realized his mare had a shot at the Derby. As he suspected, eight trainers scratched their horses from the Derby in the wake of the Blue Grass, and the field was reduced to twelve.

All fears and reservations were laid aside when Genuine Risk barreled past Plugged Nickle and Rockhill Native on the turn for home. Then Bert and Diana Firestone's gallant chestnut filly with the diminutive frame beat off Rumbo's late bid at the wire.

Her next appearance would be at Pimlico in the Preakness. It was just possible that in this year when there were no outstanding colts a filly might actually win the Triple Crown. But Genuine Risk and Vasquez, making their stretch run, were bumped and ridden out by Angel Cordero on Codex, as the country watched this obvious foul that dashed all hopes for a filly Triple Crown champ.

PLEASANT COLONY * May 2, 1981

In this oil painting Pleasant Colony blasts down the stretch toward victory with Jorge Velasquez, who would finally receive world recognition for his consistent winning career.

Derby officials had invoked a limit on the number of starters in the race which would have left Larry Barrera's Flying Nashua in his stall, and not in the starting gate at this Derby time. A court order got Flying Nashua into the race.

The day belonged to the team of Evans, Campo, Valesquez, and Pleasant Colony. In the paddock they appeared an unlikely combination: Thomas Mellon Evans, the owner, was a dignified industrialist; John Campo, the trainer, was called the "Fat Man, by Damon Runyon out of a Don Rickles Mare"; Jorge Velasquez, the jockey, was a quiet Panamanian and one of the best riders in the country; and finally there was Pleasant Colony, lop-eared, gawky, and sporting a nasty-looking skin condition on a hindquarter. He came to Churchill Downs fresh from an upset win in the Wood, where favored Cure the Blues and Proud Appeal had met each other in a speed duel that finished them both. The press latched onto the colorful Campo and gave him numerous opportunities to predict Derby victory to a national audience.

With twenty-one starters the Kentucky Derby looked like a cavalry charge as the big field swept down the stretch and past the stands for the first time. Horses were bumped and blocked, but Velasquez steered his mount clear, taking him from fifteenth after 6 furlongs to first by the top of the stretch. He held on to win by three-quarters of a length.

Up in Baltimore two weeks later, Pleasant Colony won the Preakness. But there would be no Triple Crown for Campo and Company. An outsider named Summing saw to that in the Belmont Stakes. Pleasant Colony won once more that season in the prestigious Woodward Stakes. The horse is now standing at Buckland Farm in Kentucky.

GATO DEL SOL   *   May 1, 1982

Cajun jockey Eddie Delahoussaye "works" Gato Del Sol in the morning several days prior to the 108th Derby. (Insert) Co-owners Arthur Hancock III and Leone Peters with the trophy.

In 1981 Arthur Hancock, son of the late Bull Hancock, wrote and recorded a song called "A Horse of Another Color," no doubt inspired by his gray colt. Gato Del Sol means "cat in the sun." His trainer, ex-Hollywood actor Eddie Gregson, had noticed a cat stretching and lazing in a sunny area near the stable and had decided on the Spanish translation as Gato's sire, the grass champion, Cougar II, was from Chile. Gato Del Sol joined three gray Derby winners before him—Determine, Decidedly, and Spectacular Bid.

The gray colt was a 21 to 1 long shot, the favorite being Air Forbes Won. In the early going he trailed the field of nineteen by 16 lengths and did not appear to be a threat to any horse. But in the backstretch he began to move up. Since Judge Himes in 1903, no horse has made such a move in the Derby. He came through the traffic in the turn for home and picked off his competition as he charged down the stretch. Cupecoy's Joy, the filly who led all the way, was joined by El Baba and Air Forbes Won, but all three spit out the bit at the eighth pole and the "cat in the sun" crossed the finish line 2½ lengths in front. The time for the race was a respectable 2:00⅖, and a win ticket paid $44.40, the second biggest payout since Proud Clarion in 1967.

Arthur Hancock III's father had wanted the Derby more than anything and had bred and trained horses for it all his life but never won. He came the closest in 1969 when Dike came within a half-length of Majestic Prince. At Bull Hancock's death, the executors chose his other son Seth to run Claiborne. Arthur established his own Stone Farm, just down the road, and with the help of Leone Peters, bred, among many others, Gato Del Sol. In his acceptance speech, Arthur said, "I dedicate this Derby to Daddy."

SUNNY'S HALO * May 7, 1983

Sunny's Halo and Eddie Delahoussaye with shirttails flying gallop under the wire in the 109th Kentucky Derby. A cameraman loses control in the excitement.

It was not the kind of day that Stephen Foster described. Moments before the big race as the crowd sang "My Old Kentucky Home" umbrellas went up to fend off the rain. While thousands in the infield used plastic garbage bags to keep dry, millionaires and celebrities observed the race from the climate-controlled Skye Terrace. Former presidents Gerald Ford and Jimmy Carter, Vice-President George Bush, ex-Secretary of State Henry Kissinger with Kentucky's own Governor John Y. Brown and First Lady Phyllis George Brown were there to cheer the winner across the finish line. Despite the bugs in a newly installed computer wagering system and one betting machine briefly out of commission, a crowd of 134,444 wagered a record $5,546,977, to the delight of Churchill Downs's president Lynn Stone.

Sunny's Halo out of Mostly Sunny, entered the Kentucky Derby after only 2 starts, both of which he'd won—the last on April 16 in the one and one-eighth mile Arkansas Derby with Delahoussaye in the irons for the first time.

Twenty colts started this Derby Day. Marfa, the favorite, coupled with Balboa Native and Total Departure as the Wayne Lukas entry, needed discipline according to Lukas, and it showed. He was not a threat to Sunny's Halo and Delahoussaye, who won by 2 lengths. After winning his second consecutive Derby, the first to do so since Ron Turcotte on Secretariat, Delahoussaye said, "God, it's a great feeling!"

INDEX

[*All names of horses are in italics*]

144

145